The
BATHROOM
SPORTS
ALMANAC

———— • ————

by

Jeff Kreismer

RED-LETTER PRESS, INC.
Saddle River, New Jersey

Red-Letter Press, Inc.
P.O. Box 393
Saddle River, NJ 07458

www.Red-LetterPress.com

ACKNOWLEDGMENTS

BOOK DESIGN & TYPOGRAPHY:
Jeff Kreismer

•

COVER ART:
Design by Damonza

•

EDITORIAL:
Jack Kreismer

•

RESEARCH & DEVELOPMENT:
Rachel Jackson
Kobus Reyneke

The
BATHROOM
SPORTS
ALMANAC

JANUARY

1

Today's Trivia: On January 1, 2015, what four teams took part in the first-ever College Football Playoff in two semi-final contests?

Birthdays: Hank Greenberg, 1911; Rocky Graziano, 1919; Doak Walker, 1927; LaMarr Hoyt, 1955; Derrick Thomas, 1967; Bobby Holik, 1971; Fernando Tatis, 1975; Glen Davis, 1986; Dallas Keuchel, 1988; Jason Pierre-Paul, 1989

On This Day: In 1902, the granddaddy of college football games was born. Michigan blanked Stanford, 49-0, in the inaugural Rose Bowl (then called the East-West Game). Attendance was so sparse that 14 years passed before the second game was played.

Trivia Answer: Oregon beat Florida State in the Rose Bowl, while Ohio State topped Alabama in the Sugar Bowl. Ohio State would later beat Oregon for the National Championship.

JANUARY

2

Today's Trivia: On January 2, 1989, two undefeated college football squads entered the National Championship Game. Who defeated West Virginia, 34-21, to claim its last title to date?

Birthdays: Gino Marchetti, 1927; Calvin Hill, 1947; Bill Madlock, 1951; Robbie Ftorek, 1952; David Cone, 1963; Edgar Martinez, 1963; Pernell Whitaker, 1964; Greg Swindell, 1965; Scott Mitchell, 1968; Royce Clayton, 1970; Jeff Suppan, 1975; Brian Boucher, 1977; Kirk Hinrich, 1981

On This Day: In 1965, Joe Namath signed his first contract with the New York Jets for the then-unheard of sum of $400,000. The charismatic quarterback from little Beaver Falls, PA, quickly adjusted to life in the Big Apple - especially the nightlife - earning the nickname "Broadway Joe."

Trivia Answer: Notre Dame

JANUARY

Today's Trivia: On January 3, 1993, the Bills overcame a 32-point deficit, the largest in NFL history, to win 41-38 in overtime and eliminate what team from the playoffs?

Birthdays: Hank Stram, 1923; Bobby Hull, 1939; Darren Daulton, 1962; Jim Everett, 1963; Cheryl Miller, 1964; Luis Sojo, 1966; Michael Schumacher, 1969; A.J. Burnett, 1977; David Tyree, 1980; Eli Manning, 1981

On This Day: In 1920, Babe Ruth traded in his red socks for Yankee pinstripes. Boston owner Harry Frazee dealt Ruth to New York to the everlasting dismay of Red Sox loyalists. And speaking of controversial owners: It was on this day in 1973 that George Steinbrenner purchased the Yankees from CBS.

Trivia Answer: Houston Oilers

JANUARY

Today's Trivia: On January 4, 1970, what team, who would go on to win Super Bowl IV over the Vikings, defeated the Oakland Raiders in the final American Football League Championship Game?

Birthdays: Johnny Lujack, 1925; Don Shula, 1930; Floyd Patterson, 1935; Charlie Manuel, 1944; Daryl Boston, 1963; Garrison Hearst, 1971; Ted Lilly, 1976; Al Jefferson, 1985; Eric Weddle, 1985; Kevin Pillar, 1989; Kris Bryant, 1992

On This Day: In 2006, Vince Young scored on a last-second touchdown run to give his Texas Longhorns a thrilling 41-38 win over USC in the Rose Bowl and claim the national title. Young was named the MVP with 267 yards passing, 200 yards rushing and three touchdowns. Texas' come-from-behind victory snapped a 34-game Trojans win streak.

Trivia Answer: Kansas City Chiefs (The NFL absorbed the upstart AFL the following season.)

JANUARY

5

Today's Trivia: On January 5, 1971, what
legendary sports franchise lost a game for the first time
in over eight years after 2,495 straight wins?

Birthdays: Lou Carnesecca, 1925; Chuck Noll, 1932;
Jim Otto, 1938; Chuck McKinley, 1941; Sam Wyche, 1945;
Mercury Morris, 1947; Charlie Hough, 1948; Alex English, 1954;
Danny Jackson, 1962; Warrick Dunn, 1975; Jose Iglesias, 1990

On This Day: In 1988, hoops legend "Pistol" Pete Maravich
died at the age of 40. Maravich was in the middle of a pickup
basketball game in California when he collapsed on the court from
cardiac arrest. Fifteen years earlier, Maravich eerily said, "I don't
want to play 10 years in the NBA and die of a heart attack at age 40."

Trivia Answer: The Harlem Globetrotters, who fell, 100-99, to the New Jersey Reds

---

JANUARY

6

Today's Trivia: On January 6, 2002, who fell on
Brett Favre to break the NFL's single-season sack record
with 22.5?

Birthdays: Early Wynn, 1920; Ralph Branca, 1926;
Lou Holtz, 1937; Nancy Lopez, 1957; Paul Azinger, 1960;
Howie Long, 1960; Charles Haley, 1964; Marlon Anderson, 1974;
James Farrior, 1975; Casey Fossum, 1978; Gilbert Arenas, 1982;
A.J. Hawk, 1984; Ndamukong Suh, 1987; Jameis Winston, 1994

On This Day: In 1951, Indianapolis and Rochester battled
through six overtimes before Indianapolis prevailed, 75-73. Playing
in the era before the 24-second shot clock, the teams held on to the
ball as long as possible before shooting. It remains the longest game
in NBA history.

Trivia Answer: Michael Strahan

JANUARY

Today's Trivia: On January 7, 1992, Tom Seaver was elected to the Baseball Hall of Fame with a record 98.8% of the vote by the Baseball Writers' Association of America. His mark would stand until 2016, when who topped him with 99.3% of the vote?

Birthdays: Johnny Mize, 1913; Alvin Dark, 1922; Eddie LeBaron, 1930; Tony Conigliaro, 1945; Jeff Montgomery, 1962; Ron Rivera, 1962; Eric Gagne, 1976; Alfonso Soriano, 1976; Kevin Mench, 1978; Francisco Rodriguez, 1982; Edwin Encarnacion, 1983; Natalie Gulbis, 1983; Jon Lester, 1984; Michael Sam, 1990

On This Day: In 1972, the Los Angeles Lakers defeated the Atlanta Hawks, 134-90, for their 33rd consecutive win, an NBA record that still stands today. They would finish the season with 69 wins and a championship.

Trivia Answer: Ken Griffey Jr.

JANUARY

Today's Trivia: On January 8, 1955, Georgia Tech snapped the 129-game home winning streak of what college hoops squad coached by the legendary Adolph Rupp?

Birthdays: Bruce Sutter, 1953; Dwight Clark, 1957; Calvin Natt, 1957; Jason Giambi, 1971; Mike Cameron, 1973; Carl Pavano, 1976; Jeff Francis, 1981; Jeff Francoeur, 1984

On This Day: In 2000, the Music City Miracle took place when the Titans beat the Bills in the playoffs. A Frank Wycheck lateral allowed Kevin Dyson to score the game-winning touchdown off the kickoff after Buffalo had just taken the lead with seconds left. Exactly 12 years later, the Broncos experienced their own playoff miracle when Tim Tebow hit Demaryius Thomas for an 80-yard score to beat the Steelers in overtime.

Trivia Answer: Kentucky Wildcats

JANUARY

9

Today's Trivia: On January 9, 2000, Dan Marino recorded the final victory of his NFL career when his Dolphins beat the Seahawks in the last game ever played at what venue?

Birthdays: Bart Starr, 1934; Dick Enberg, 1935; Ralph Terry, 1936; M.L. Carr, 1951; Otis Nixon, 1959; Stan Javier, 1964; Muggsy Bogues, 1965; Chad Johnson, 1978; Sergio Garcia, 1980

On This Day: In 1942, Joe Louis KO'd Buddy Baer in the first round of their heavyweight championship bout. "The Brown Bomber" donated his entire $76,000 purse to the wartime relief effort.

Trivia Answer: The Kingdome in Seattle

JANUARY

10

Today's Trivia: On January 10, 1982, what 49er made "The Catch", the winning score that beat the Cowboys in the NFC title game and sent the 49ers to the Super Bowl?

Birthdays: Frank Mahovlich, 1938; Willie McCovey, 1938; Bill Toomey, 1939; George Foreman, 1949; Richard Dotson, 1959; Glenn Robinson, 1973; Adam Kennedy, 1976

On This Day: In 1982, the Cincinnati Bengals iced the AFC championship with a 27-7 win over the San Diego Chargers. More notable than the score were the temperature (nine below zero) and the wind chill (59 below), making this "Freezer Bowl" the coldest playoff game on record.

Trivia Answer: Dwight Clark

JANUARY

Today's Trivia: On January 11, 1987, John Elway led his Broncos on "The Drive", marching 98 yards for a touchdown and ultimately beating what team in the AFC Championship Game?

Birthdays: Schoolboy Rowe, 1910; Don Mossi, 1929; Ben Crenshaw, 1952; Freddie Solomon, 1953; Darryl Dawkins, 1957; Lloyd McClendon, 1959; Tracy Caulkins, 1963; Rey Ordonez, 1971; Tony Allen, 1982

On This Day: In 1973, the American League adopted the designated hitter rule as an experiment. After a three-year trial period, the DH became a permanent part of the AL batting order.

Trivia Answer: Cleveland Browns

JANUARY

Today's Trivia: On January 12, 1975, the Pittsburgh Steelers claimed their first Super Bowl title by beating the Vikings. The game's MVP ran for more yards than the entire Minnesota offense produced. Who was it?

Birthdays: Joe Frazier, 1944; Tom Dempsey, 1947; Randy Jones, 1950; Campy Russell, 1952; Dominique Wilkins, 1960; Marian Hossa, 1979; Dontrelle Willis, 1982; Ivan Nova, 1987; Claude Giroux, 1988; Justin Houston, 1989

On This Day: In 1969, the Jets' $400,000 investment in Joe Namath matured. The New Yorkers - almost three touchdown underdogs - made good on their outspoken quarterback's guarantee of victory and shocked the Baltimore Colts, 16-7, in Super Bowl III.

Trivia Answer: Franco Harris

JANUARY

13

Today's Trivia: On January 13, 1999, Michael Jordan retired from basketball for the second time. With what NBA franchise would Jordan become a part-owner and President of Basketball Operations the following year?

Birthdays: Tom Gola, 1933; Bob Baffert, 1953; Mark O'Meara, 1957; Kelly Hrudey, 1961; Kevin Mitchell, 1962; Nikolai Khabibulin, 1973; Doug Martin, 1989; Connor McDavid, 1997

On This Day: In 1982, Henry Aaron and Frank Robinson were elected to the Baseball Hall of Fame. The sluggers tallied a combined 1,341 career home runs and 4,109 RBIs.

Trivia Answer: Washington Wizards

JANUARY

14

Today's Trivia: On January 14, 1973, the Miami Dolphins defeated the Washington Redskins 14-7 to win Super Bowl VII and become the first NFL team to go undefeated. While Bob Griese was the Super Bowl starter, what other quarterback won nine games for Miami that season?

Birthdays: Sonny Siebert, 1937; Gene Washington, 1947; Carl Weathers, 1948; Swen Nater, 1950; Vincent Jackson, 1983; Erick Aybar, 1984; Hakeem Nicks, 1988

On This Day: In 1968, Green Bay legend Vince Lombardi coached his last game with the Packers, a 33-14 win over the Oakland Raiders in Super Bowl II. Lombardi spent one more year on the sidelines, with the Washington Redskins, before dying of cancer in 1970.

Trivia Answer: Earl Morrall

JANUARY

15

Today's Trivia: On January 15, 1990, with .1 seconds remaining, what Knick got off a three-pointer that beat the Bulls and ultimately led the NBA to make a rule change in his name?

Birthdays: Mike Marshall, 1943; Bobby Grich, 1949; Ernie DiGregorio, 1951; Randy White, 1953; Bernard Hopkins, 1965; Delino DeShields, 1969; Mary Pierce, 1975; Drew Brees, 1979; Matt Holliday, 1980; Armando Galarraga, 1982

On This Day: In 1967, the Green Bay Packers beat the Kansas City Chiefs, 35-10, in the first game between champions of the NFL and AFL - or Super Bowl I. Bart Starr earned MVP honors.

Trivia Answer: Trent Tucker (0.3 needs to be on the clock in order for a player to get a shot off)

JANUARY

16

Today's Trivia: On January 16, 1970, what Cardinals center fielder filed a historic lawsuit against Major League Baseball that ultimately paved the way for the beginning of free agency?

Birthdays: Dizzy Dean, 1910; A.J. Foyt, 1935; Jack McDowell, 1966; Roy Jones, Jr., 1969; Joe Horn, 1972; Albert Pujols, 1980; Joe Flacco, 1985; Mark Trumbo, 1986; Matt Duchene, 1991

On This Day: In 1972, the Dallas Cowboys earned their first Super Bowl victory with a 24-3 win over the Miami Dolphins. In the loss, the Dolphins became the only team not to score a touchdown in the history of the game.

Trivia Answer: Curt Flood

JANUARY

17

Today's Trivia: On January 17, 1999, what Minnesota Viking, who did not miss a single kick the entire regular season, wound up costing his team a trip to the Super Bowl when he missed a fourth quarter field goal against the Falcons?

Birthdays: Jacques Plante, 1929; Don Zimmer, 1931; Kip Keino, 1940; Muhammad Ali, 1942; Darrell Porter, 1952; Ted Thompson, 1953; Chili Davis, 1960; Jeremy Roenick, 1970; Derrick Mason, 1974; Dwyane Wade, 1982; Trevor Bauer, 1991

On This Day: In 1916, the Professional Golfers Association was founded and made its debut later that year at the Siwanoy Country Club in Bronxville, NY.

Trivia Answer: Gary Anderson

JANUARY

18

Today's Trivia: On January 18, 2015, the Patriots advanced to the Super Bowl, but not without controversy. Against what postseason victim did New England's infamous "Deflategate" scandal occur?

Birthdays: Curt Flood, 1938; Scott McGregor, 1954; Mark Messier, 1961; Brady Anderson, 1964; Mike Lieberthal, 1972; Wandy Rodriguez, 1979; Julius Peppers, 1980; Michael Pineda, 1989; Brett Lawrie, 1990

On This Day: In 1983, the International Olympic Committee cleared Jim Thorpe's name. Replicas of the gold decathlon and pentathlon medals from the 1912 Games were presented to his heirs. Thorpe had been stripped of the awards because of allegations that he had forfeited his amateur status by taking money to play baseball.

Trivia Answer: Indianapolis Colts

JANUARY

19

Today's Trivia: On January 19, 2002, the Patriots snuck past the Raiders in a snowy Divisional Playoff Game. New England was aided by a call in which a Tom Brady fumble was changed to an incomplete pass as a result of what obscure (and now infamous) rule?

Birthdays: Bill Mlkvy, 1931; Joe Schmidt, 1932; Dan Reeves, 1944; Jon Matlack, 1950; Ottis Anderson, 1957; Chris Sabo, 1962; Jeff Van Gundy, 1962; Michael Adams, 1963; Stefan Edberg, 1966; Junior Seau, 1969; Phil Nevin, 1971; Walter Jones, 1974; Johnny Boychuk, 1984; Shawn Johnson, 1992

On This Day: In 1974, Notre Dame shocked UCLA, 71-70, to end the Bruins consecutive game winning streak at 88, the longest in NCAA college basketball history.

Trivia Answer: The Tuck Rule

JANUARY

20

Today's Trivia: On January 20, 1991, what NFC team advanced to the Super Bowl with a game-winning field goal before doing the same (this time, in overtime) on January 20, 2008?

Birthdays: Camilo Pascual, 1934; Carol Heiss, 1940; Ozzie Guillen, 1964; Ron Harper, 1964; Chris Morris, 1966; Mark Stepnoski, 1967; Nick Anderson, 1968; Brian Giles, 1971; David Eckstein, 1975; Jason Richardson, 1981; Geovany Soto, 1983; Nick Foles, 1989

On This Day: In 1968, the University of Houston ended UCLA's 47-game winning streak, defeating the Bruins, 71-69. The Game of the Century, showcasing Elvin Hayes and Lew Alcindor, was the first nationally televised college basketball game.

Trivia Answer: New York Giants (They beat the 49ers and Packers, respectively.)

JANUARY

Today's Trivia: On January 21, 1992, who became just the second head coach of the Pittsburgh Steelers since 1969, when Chuck Noll was hired?

Birthdays: John Chaney, 1932; Jack Nicklaus, 1940; Johnny Oates, 1946; Mike Krukow, 1952; Hakeem Olajuwon, 1963; Detlef Schrempf, 1963; Dalton Hilliard, 1964; Rusty Greer, 1969; Dany Heatley, 1981; Haloti Ngata, 1984; Jonathan Quick, 1986; Brandon Crawford, 1987; Ashton Eaton, 1988

On This Day: In 1975, women were allowed to go where no female had gone before - the players' locker room. Officials at the NHL All-Star Game adopted an open door policy that marked the first time in pro sports history that reporters of both sexes had access to this steamy sanctuary.

Trivia Answer: Bill Cowher

JANUARY

Today's Trivia: On January 22, 2006, Kobe Bryant scored 81 points in a Lakers win over the Raptors. Who was the last player to top the 70-point mark in an NBA game before Kobe?

Birthdays: Elmer Lach, 1918; Joe Perry, 1927; George Seifert, 1940; Serge Savard, 1946; Mike Bossy, 1957; Chone Figgins, 1978; Carlos Ruiz, 1979; Jason Peters, 1982; Ubaldo Jimenez, 1984; Ray Rice, 1987; Greg Oden, 1988

On This Day: In 1973, George Foreman pummeled Joe Frazier to capture the heavyweight crown with a second-round TKO in Kingston, Jamaica. Foreman reigned for 21 months before being dethroned by Muhammad Ali.

Trivia Answer: David Robinson, in 1994

JANUARY

23

Today's Trivia: On January 23, 1983, the Dolphins defeated the Jets, 14-0, in the AFC Championship Game. The contest earned what nickname due to its less-than-desirable playing conditions?

Birthdays: Chico Carrasquel, 1928; Jerry Kramer, 1936; Kurt Bevacqua, 1947; Pat Haden, 1953; Eric Metcalf, 1968; Brendan Shanahan, 1969; Alan Embree, 1970; Mark Wohlers, 1970; Julie Foudy, 1971; Kevin Mawae, 1971; Jeff Samardzija, 1985; Addison Russell, 1994

On This Day: In 1944, the Detroit Red Wings set NHL records for the most goals, most consecutive goals, and most points in a game (37) as they lambasted the New York Rangers, 15-0.

Trivia Answer: The Mud Bowl

JANUARY

24

Today's Trivia: On January 24, 1999, what golfer made PGA history when he shot a 59 in the final round en route to winning the Bob Hope Chrysler Classic?

Birthdays: Mark Eaton, 1957; Atlee Hammaker, 1958; Rob Dibble, 1964; Mary Lou Retton, 1968; Chris Warren, 1968; Scott Kazmir, 1984; Jose Quintana, 1989

On This Day: In 1981, Mike Bossy became the second player in NHL history (after Maurice Richard) to score 50 goals in 50 games. He did so by scoring twice with less than five minutes remaining in the Islanders' 50th game of the season. Exactly five years later, Bossy would notch his 1,000th career point.

Trivia Answer: David Duval

JANUARY

Today's Trivia: On January 25, 1924, the very first Winter Olympics began. What country had the honor of hosting the Games?

Birthdays: Ernie Harwell, 1918; Lou "The Toe" Groza, 1924; Dick McGuire, 1926; Don Maynard, 1935; Eusébio, 1942; Mark Duper, 1959; Chris Chelios, 1962; Derrick Turnbow, 1978; Patrick Willis, 1985; Danny Woodhead, 1985

On This Day: In 1987, the New York Giants defeated the Denver Broncos, 39-20, to win their first Super Bowl. Game MVP Phil Simms set a record by going 22 of 25 passing. He threw for 304 yards and three touchdowns.

Trivia Answer: France (Chamonix)

JANUARY

Today's Trivia: On January 26, 1986, the Bears pummeled the Patriots to win Super Bowl XX. What XXL lineman ran in a late score to increase Chicago's lead to 41 points?

Birthdays: Bob Uecker, 1935; Jack Youngblood, 1950; Wayne Gretzky, 1961; Curtis Duncan, 1965; Vince Carter, 1977; Hector Noesi, 1987; Torrey Smith, 1989; Manti Te'o, 1991

On This Day: In 1960, Danny Heater of Burnsville, WV, scored 135 points in a 32-minute high school basketball game. With Heater accounting for almost 80% of their offense and pulling down 32 rebounds, Burnsville "edged" Widen, 173-43.

Trivia Answer: William "Refrigerator" Perry

JANUARY

27

Today's Trivia: On January 27, 1991, whose "wide right" 47-yard field goal attempt enabled the Giants to hold on for a 20-19 win over the Bills in Super Bowl XXV?

Birthdays: Fritz Pollard, 1894; Art Rooney, 1901; Cris Collinsworth, 1959; Phil Plantier, 1969; Fred Taylor, 1976; Angel Berroa, 1978; Marat Safin, 1980; Gavin Floyd, 1983; Julio Teheran, 1991

On This Day: In 1944, Casey Stengel was fired as manager of the Boston Braves after five successive losing seasons. He fared a little better in his next major league managing assignment, piloting the Yankees to 10 pennants and seven world championships.

Trivia Answer: Scott Norwood

JANUARY

28

Today's Trivia: On January 28, 2005, after 13 seasons with the Cubs, Sammy Sosa was traded to what American League squad?

Birthdays: Parry O'Brien, 1932; Bill White, 1934; Gregg Popovich, 1949; Colin Campbell, 1953; Nick Price, 1957; Tony Delk, 1974; Jermaine Dye, 1974; Magglio Ordonez, 1974; Daunte Culpepper, 1977; Lyle Overbay, 1977; Andre Iguodala, 1984

On This Day: In 1958, Roy Campanella's career was ended by a car crash that left him paralyzed. In his 10 years as the Brooklyn backstop, Campy was the National League MVP three times, helping to lead the Dodgers to five pennants and one world championship.

Trivia Answer: Baltimore Orioles

JANUARY

Today's Trivia: On January 29, 1995, what quarterback set a Super Bowl record with six passing touchdowns in his team's 49-26 victory?

Birthdays: Pat Quinn, 1943; Greg Louganis, 1960; Steve Sax, 1960; Andre Reed, 1964; Dominik Hasek, 1965; Sean Burke, 1967; Aeneas Williams, 1968; Jason Schmidt, 1973; Marc Gasol, 1985; Jair Jurrjens, 1986; Jose Abreu, 1987; Alex Avila, 1987

On This Day: In 2012, Novak Djokovic outlasted Rafael Nadal in the Australian Open in the longest singles final, time-wise, in Grand Slam history. The 5 hour, 53 minute classic ended with Djokovic claiming a third consecutive Grand Slam win over his rival.

Trivia Answer: Steve Young, whose 49ers beat the Chargers in Super Bowl XXIX

JANUARY

Today's Trivia: On January 30, 1983, the Redskins defeated the Dolphins in Super Bowl XVII. Because Washington's owner had already won the NBA crown in 1972 with the Lakers, he became the first person to own title-winning franchises in two major sports. What's his name?

Birthdays: Charlie Neal, 1931; Davey Johnson, 1943; Tom Izzo, 1955; Curtis Strange, 1955; Payne Stewart, 1957; Jalen Rose, 1973; Cameron Wake, 1982; Jeremy Hermida, 1984

On This Day: In 1996, Magic Johnson made his return. He played in his first NBA game since announcing his retirement in 1991 after becoming HIV-positive. Magic put up 19 points, 10 assists and 8 rebounds off the bench as his Lakers defeated the Warriors, 128-118.

Trivia Answer: Jack Kent Cooke

JANUARY

Today's Trivia: On January 31, 1999, what quarterback became the oldest Super Bowl MVP after his team won it all in his final NFL game?

Birthdays: Don Hutson, 1913; Jackie Robinson, 1919; Ernie Banks, 1931; Nolan Ryan, 1947; Yuniesky Betancourt, 1982; Vernon Davis, 1984; Josh Johnson, 1984; Mario Williams, 1985; Tyler Seguin, 1992

On This Day: In 1988, the Redskins dominated the Broncos, 42-10, in Super Bowl XXII. Exactly five years later, the Cowboys destroyed the Bills, 52-17, in SB XXVII. Quarterbacks Doug Williams and Troy Aikman earned respective MVP honors.

Trivia Answer: John Elway, at age 38
(The Broncos beat the Falcons, 34-19, in Super Bowl XXXIII.)

FEBRUARY

Today's Trivia: On February 1, 1970, what New York Ranger recorded the 103rd and final shutout of his legendary career?

Birthdays: Conn Smythe, 1895; Paul Blair, 1944; Wade Wilson, 1959; Michelle Akers, 1966; Kent Mercker, 1968; Malik Sealy, 1970; Tommy Salo, 1971; Kevin Martin, 1983; Austin Jackson, 1987; Ronda Rousey, 1987; Brett Anderson, 1988

On This Day: In 2015, the Patriots won Super Bowl XLIX, 28-24, after one of the game's most unbelievable finishes. Rookie Malcolm Butler intercepted Seattle's Russell Wilson on New England's one-yard line with seconds left. Exactly 11 years earlier, the Pats won Super Bowl XXXVIII over the Panthers in another thriller, 32-29. Tom Brady claimed both MVPs.

Trivia Answer: Terry Sawchuk

FEBRUARY

Today's Trivia: On February 2, 2012, what
Edmonton Oiler recorded four goals and four assists
against the Chicago Blackhawks, becoming the first player
with eight or more points in a game since 1989?

Birthdays: George Halas, 1895; Red Schoendienst, 1923; Bob
Richards, 1926; Wayne Fontes, 1940; Arturs Irbe, 1967; Sean Elliott,
1968; Scott Erickson, 1968; Melvin Mora, 1972; Todd Bertuzzi, 1975;
Donald Driver, 1975; Adam Everett, 1977; American Pharoah, 2012

On This Day: In 1936, the inaugural Baseball Hall of Fame
election results were announced. The first inductees were Ty Cobb,
Walter Johnson, Christy Mathewson, Babe Ruth and Honus Wagner.

Trivia Answer: Sam Gagner

FEBRUARY

Today's Trivia: On February 3, 1989, what
Yankees broadcaster was named President of the National
League, becoming the first African-American to head a major
pro sports league?

Birthdays: Emile Griffith, 1938; Fran Tarkenton, 1940;
Bob Griese, 1945; Fred Lynn, 1952; Vlade Divac, 1968;
Retief Goosen, 1969; Skip Schumaker, 1980; Lucas Duda, 1986;
Julio Jones, 1989; Rougned Odor, 1994

On This Day: In 2008, the New York Giants shocked the
football world and the undefeated Patriots, beating New England,
17-14, in Super Bowl XLII. Six years earlier to the day, the Pats
pulled off their own stunner when they won their first title with
a 20-17 win over the Rams in Super Bowl XXXVI.

Trivia Answer: Bill White

FEBRUARY

Today's Trivia: On February 4, 2007, the Colts defeated the Bears, 29-17, to win Super Bowl XLI. What weather-related phenomenon was unique about the game?

Birthdays: Byron Nelson, 1912; Lawrence Taylor, 1959; Denis Savard, 1961; Dan Plesac, 1962; Jerome Brown, 1965; Oscar De La Hoya, 1973; Doug Fister, 1984

On This Day: In 1991, the Baseball Hall of Fame voted to ban Pete Rose for life. On this date in 1997, in another off the field decision, O.J. Simpson was found to be civilly liable for the deaths of Nicole Brown Simpson and Ronald Goldman.

Trivia Answer: It was the first time that rain fell throughout the Super Bowl.

FEBRUARY

Today's Trivia: On February 5, 1989, the NBA's all-time leading scorer became the first (and only) player to top the 38,000-point mark. Who is he?

Birthdays: Hank Aaron, 1934; Roger Staubach, 1942; Craig Morton, 1943; Darrell Waltrip, 1947; Roberto Alomar, 1968; Eric O'Flaherty, 1985; Cristiano Ronaldo, 1985; Neymar, 1992

On This Day: In 2006, the Pittsburgh Steelers defeated the Seattle Seahawks, 21-10, to win Super Bowl XL. Hines Ward was the MVP as the Steelers won the big game for the fifth time, tying the Cowboys and 49ers for the most Super Bowl victories.

Trivia Answer: Kareem Abdul-Jabbar

FEBRUARY

Today's Trivia: On February 6, 1993, the world lost a tennis legend – the only African-American man to win Wimbledon and the U.S. and Australian Opens. Who?

Birthdays: Babe Ruth, 1895; Dale Long, 1926; Smoky Burgess, 1927; Richie Zisk, 1949; Bob Wickman, 1969; Kris Humphries, 1985; Pedro Alvarez, 1987; Travis Wood, 1987; Jermaine Kearse, 1990

On This Day: In 2011, the Packers defeated the Steelers, 31-25, in Super Bowl XLV. Over 100,000 were on hand at Cowboys Stadium to see Green Bay claim their fourth Super Bowl victory. Aaron Rodgers, with 304 yards passing and three touchdowns, was named MVP.

Trivia Answer: Arthur Ashe, who died at 49 from complications of AIDS

FEBRUARY

Today's Trivia: On February 7, 1970, Pete Maravich poured in 69 points against Alabama as a member of what school's team?

Birthdays: Dan Quisenberry, 1953; Damaso Garcia, 1957; Carney Lansford, 1957; Juwan Howard, 1973; Steve Nash, 1974; David Aebischer, 1978; Endy Chavez, 1978; Scott Feldman, 1983; Matthew Stafford, 1988; Isaiah Thomas, 1989; Steven Stamkos, 1990; Roberto Osuna, 1995

On This Day: In 1976, Darryl Sittler had the hot hand on the ice, setting an NHL record for points in a game. Sittler scored six goals and added four assists in Toronto's 11-4 win over Boston.

Trivia Answer: Louisiana State University

FEBRUARY

Today's Trivia: On February 8, 1986, what 5'7" player won the NBA's Slam Dunk Contest by defeating teammate Dominique Wilkins?

Birthdays: Clete Boyer, 1937; Fritz Peterson, 1942; Joe Maddon, 1954; John Fox, 1955; Raleigh & Reggie McKenzie, 1955; Marques Johnson, 1956; Dino Ciccarelli, 1960; Alonzo Mourning, 1970; Aaron Cook, 1979; Klay Thompson, 1990

On This Day: In 1936, in an effort to offset the dominance of the Giants and Bears, the NFL conducted the first college draft. The Eagles used the first pick to select University of Chicago running back Jay Berwanger.

Trivia Answer: Spud Webb

FEBRUARY

Today's Trivia: On February 9, 2003, Michael Jordan played in his final NBA All-Star Game. While MJ wasn't voted in by the fans, what Toronto Raptor gave up his spot to allow Jordan to start the game?

Birthdays: Dit Clapper, 1907; Bill Veeck, 1914; Clete Boyer, 1937; Danny White, 1952; Mookie Wilson, 1956; John Kruk, 1961; Jimmy Smith, 1969; Vladimir Guerrero, 1975; Dioner Navarro, 1984

On This Day: In 1971, Leroy "Satchel" Paige became the first member of the Negro League to be inducted into the Baseball Hall of Fame. Although his career Major League record was only 28-31, Paige laid claim to 2,500 appearances in the Negro League.

Trivia Answer: Vince Carter

FEBRUARY

Today's Trivia: On February 10, 2002, what player heard boos from the crowd as he was named the NBA All-Star Game MVP in his hometown of Philadelphia?

Birthdays: Herb Pennock, 1894; Allie Reynolds, 1917; Mark Spitz, 1950; Greg Norman, 1955; John Calipari, 1959; Lenny Dykstra, 1963; Daryl Johnston, 1966; Ty Law, 1974; Hiroki Kuroda, 1975; Lance Berkman, 1976; Mike Ribeiro, 1980; Justin Gatlin, 1982; Alex Gordon, 1984; Paul Millsap, 1985; Travis d'Arnaud, 1989; C. J. Anderson, 1991

On This Day: In 1968, Peggy Fleming won the women's figure skating gold medal at Grenoble, France. Fleming earned every first place vote from the judges in giving the U.S. its only gold in the Winter Olympics that year.

Trivia Answer: Kobe Bryant

FEBRUARY

Today's Trivia: On February 11, 1997, what legend was introduced as the new head coach of the New York Jets, a one-win team he would go on to lead to a winning record?

Birthdays: Max Baer, 1909; Eddie Shack, 1937; Sammy Ellis, 1941; Ben Oglivie, 1949; Todd Benzinger, 1963; Ben McLemore, 1993

On This Day: In 1990, journeyman heavyweight James "Buster" Douglas knocked Mike Tyson and the boxing world for a loop with a 10th round knockout of the formerly undefeated champ. The unheralded Douglas entered the fight as a 42-1 underdog.

Trivia Answer: Bill Parcells

FEBRUARY

12

Today's Trivia: On February 12, 1937, Cleveland was granted an NFL franchise. The team, still in existence today, would play in Ohio until 1946, when they moved to Los Angeles. Who are they?

Birthdays: Dom DiMaggio, 1917; Joe Garagiola, 1926; Bill Russell, 1934; Chet Lemon, 1955; Larry Nance, 1959; Brent Jones, 1963; Owen Nolan, 1972; Brad Keselowski, 1984; Todd Frazier, 1986; DeMarco Murray, 1988; Robert Griffin III, 1990; Paxton Lynch, 1994

On This Day: In 1994, the opening ceremonies were held for the 17th Olympic Winter Games in Lillehammer, Norway. This was the first time that the Winter and Summer Games did not take place in the same year. The Norwegians would take home the most medals, 26.

Trivia Answer: Rams

FEBRUARY

13

Today's Trivia: On February 13, 1994, what Temple head coach infamously threatened UMass' John Calipari in the middle of a press conference?

Birthdays: Patty Berg, 1918; Eddie Robinson, 1919; Sal Bando, 1944; Mike Krzyzewski, 1947; Donnie Moore, 1954; Marc Crawford, 1961; Mats Sundin, 1971; Randy Moss, 1977; Drew Henson, 1980; Michael Turner, 1982; Nathan Eovaldi, 1990

On This Day: In 1954, Frank Selvy scored an even 100 points for an NCAA Division I record in a 149-95 victory over Newberry. Selvy hit on 41 field goals and 18 free throws, his last score coming on a desperation heave near mid-court at the buzzer.

Trivia Answer: John Chaney

FEBRUARY

Today's Trivia: On February 14, 1990, Michael Jordan was forced to wear what number for the one and only time in his career after his #23 was stolen from the locker room before the game?

Birthdays: Mel Allen, 1913; Woody Hayes, 1913; Mickey Wright, 1935; Dave Dravecky, 1956; Jim Kelly, 1960; Takashi Saito, 1970; Drew Bledsoe, 1972; Steve McNair, 1973; Milan Hejduk, 1976; Richard Hamilton, 1978; Brad Halsey, 1981; Tyler Clippard, 1985; Derek Norris, 1989; Alshon Jeffery, 1990; Jadeveon Clowney, 1993; Christian Hackenberg, 1995

On This Day: In 1951, Sugar Ray Robinson knocked out Jake LaMotta to gain the middleweight title. Robinson went on to lose the crown to Randy Turpin, only to regain the title that same year.

Trivia Answer: 12

FEBRUARY

Today's Trivia: On February 15, 1998, "The Intimidator" won his first and only Daytona 500. Who is he?

Birthdays: John Hadl, 1940; Ron Cey, 1948; Ken Anderson, 1949; Darrell Green, 1960; Mark Price, 1964; Jaromir Jagr, 1972; Amy Van Dyken, 1973; Ugueth Urbina, 1974; Alex Gonzalez, 1977; Russell Martin, 1983; Johnny Cueto, 1986; Jarryd Hayne, 1988

On This Day: In 1978, Leon Spinks won a stunning 15-round split decision over Muhammad Ali, becoming the heavyweight champ in just his eighth professional fight. It was the fastest-ever ascent to the title.

Trivia Answer: Dale Earnhardt

FEBRUARY

Today's Trivia: On February 16, 1984, who became the first American man to win an Olympic gold medal in downhill skiing?

Birthdays: Herb Williams, 1958; John McEnroe, 1959; Kelly Tripucka, 1959; Jerome Bettis, 1972; Eric Byrnes, 1976; Ahman Green, 1977

On This Day: In 2005, Commissioner Gary Bettman canceled the 2004-05 NHL season. This was the first time that a North American professional sports league canceled an entire season due to a labor dispute.

Trivia Answer: Bill Johnson

FEBRUARY

Today's Trivia: On February 17, 1968, what sports Hall of Fame opened its doors in Springfield, Massachusetts?

Birthdays: Wally Pipp, 1893; Red Barber, 1908; Buddy Ryan, 1934; Jim Brown, 1936; Dennis Green, 1949; Michael Jordan, 1963; Luc Robitaille, 1966; Tommy Moe, 1970; Scott Williamson, 1976; Josh Willingham, 1979

On This Day: In 2014, American ice dancing pair Charlie White and Meryl Davis took home the gold medal during the Sochi Winter Olympics. It was the first gold ever won by the U.S. in the sport.

Trivia Answer: Naismith Memorial Basketball Hall of Fame

FEBRUARY 18

Today's Trivia: On February 18, 1986, what Spurs guard recorded the second quadruple-double in NBA history with a stat line of 20 points, 11 rebounds, 10 assists and 10 steals?

Birthdays: George Gipp, 1895; Joe Gordon, 1915; Dick Duff, 1936; Manny Mota, 1938; Judy Rankin, 1945; John Mayberry, 1949; Andy Moog, 1960; Kevin Tapani, 1964; John Valentin, 1967; Andrei Kirilenko, 1981; Alexis Rios, 1981; Didi Gregorius, 1990; Le'Veon Bell, 1992

On This Day: In 1979, Richard Petty drove his Oldsmobile an average of 143.977 mph to become the first man to win the Daytona 500 six times. Petty went on to take a seventh victory lap at Daytona before his retirement in 1992.

Trivia Answer: Alvin Robertson (Nate Thurmond had the first.)

FEBRUARY 19

Today's Trivia: On February 19, 1996, goaltender Patrick Roy won his 300th NHL game. While Roy would retire with the most wins in league history, his record would ultimately be smashed by what netminder?

Birthdays: Eddie Arcaro, 1916; Bobby Unser, 1934; Paul Krause, 1942; Dave Stewart, 1957; Roger Goodell, 1959; Hanna Mandlikova, 1962; Miguel Batista, 1971; Dwight Freeney, 1980; Mike Miller, 1980

On This Day: In 1984, twins Phil and Steve Mahre finished first and second in the slalom at the Winter Olympics in Sarajevo, Yugoslavia. Phil turned in the better overall time to capture the gold.

Trivia Answer: Martin Brodeur (691 wins vs. Roy's 551)

FEBRUARY

Today's Trivia: On February 20, 1998, what 15-year-old became the youngest gold medalist in women's figure skating history at the Winter Games in Nagano, Japan?

Birthdays: Roy Face, 1928; Roger Penske, 1937; Phil Esposito, 1942; Charles Barkley, 1963; Noureddine Morceli, 1970; Livan Hernandez, 1975; Stephon Marbury, 1977; Ryan Langerhans, 1980; Justin Verlander, 1983; Brian McCann, 1984; Jurickson Profar, 1993; Luis Severino, 1994

On This Day: In 1988, Boitano bested Orser in the "Battle of the Brians" at the Winter Olympics in Calgary. American Brian Boitano's performance in the free skate program proved to be the margin of victory over Canadian Brian Orser for the gold medal in figure skating.

Trivia Answer: Tara Lipinski

FEBRUARY

Today's Trivia: On February 21, 2003, who became the first 40-year-old in NBA history to score 40 points in a single game?

Birthdays: Jack Ramsay, 1925; Alan Trammell, 1958; Terry Allen, 1968; Brian Rolston, 1973; Steve Francis, 1977; Tsuyoshi Wada, 1981; Franklin Gutierrez, 1983

On This Day: In 1952, men's figure skater Dick Button won his second Olympic gold medal after performing the first triple jump in competition. Button won his first gold in 1948, when he was credited with the first successful double axel jump in competition.

Trivia Answer: Michael Jordan (43)

FEBRUARY

22

Today's Trivia: On February 22, 1988, what decorated Olympian won speed skating gold in the women's 500 meters with a world record time of 39.10 seconds?

Birthdays: Connie Mack, 1862; Charlie Finley, 1918; Sparky Anderson, 1934; Julius Erving, 1950; Amy Alcott, 1956; Vijay Singh, 1963; Pat LaFontaine, 1965; Kazuhiro Sasaki, 1968; Jayson Williams, 1968; Michael Chang, 1972; J.J. Putz, 1977; Casey Kotchman, 1983; Daniel Nava, 1983; Rajon Rondo, 1986; Khalil Mack, 1991

On This Day: In 1980, the "Miracle on Ice" took place in Lake Placid, NY. The U.S. Olympic hockey team upset the heavily favored Soviets, 4-3, to advance to the finals against Finland. The Soviet Union had won the gold in the four previous Olympics.

Trivia Answer: Bonnie Blair

FEBRUARY

23

Today's Trivia: On February 23, 1985, what college hoops coach displayed his temper by infamously hurling a red chair across the Assembly Hall floor in protest of a call?

Birthdays: Elston Howard, 1929; Dante Lavelli, 1923; Tom Osborne, 1937; Fred Biletnikoff, 1943; Ed "Too Tall" Jones, 1951; Flip Saunders, 1955; Bobby Bonilla, 1963; Rondell White, 1972; Charles Tillman, 1981; Andrew Wiggins, 1995; D'Angelo Russell, 1996

On This Day: In 1980, at the Winter Olympics in Lake Placid, Eric Heiden won the 5,000-meter speed skating event for his fifth gold medal and fifth world record.

Trivia Answer: Indiana's Bob Knight

FEBRUARY

24

Today's Trivia: On February 24, 1994, the Atlanta Hawks dealt future Hall of Famer Dominique Wilkins to the L.A. Clippers in exchange for the #1 pick of the 1988 NBA Draft. Who?

Birthdays: Honus Wagner, 1874; Mike Fratello, 1947; Eddie Murray, 1956; Jeff Garcia, 1970; Mike Lowell, 1974; Zach Johnson, 1976; Bronson Arroyo, 1977; Floyd Mayweather, 1977; Lleyton Hewitt, 1981

On This Day: In 1985, quarterback Jim Kelly of the USFL's Houston Gamblers set a pro football record, passing for 574 yards in a win over Steve Young and the Los Angeles Express. Kelly's throwing exhibition also included five touchdown passes.

Trivia Answer: Danny Manning

FEBRUARY

25

Today's Trivia: On February 25, 1986, what NBA All-Star did commissioner David Stern ban for life for violating the league's drug policy?

Birthdays: Bert Bell, 1895; Bobby Riggs, 1918; Monte Irvin, 1919; Jerry Reinsdorf, 1936; Ron Santo, 1940; Carl Eller, 1942; Lee Evans, 1947; James Brown, 1951; Cesar Cedeno, 1951; Bob Brenly, 1954; Jeff Fisher, 1958; Paul O'Neill, 1963; Don Majkowski, 1964; Shannon Stewart, 1974; Joakim Noah, 1985; Jimmer Fredette, 1989; Jorge Soler, 1992

On This Day: In 1964, Muhammad Ali - then fighting as Cassius Clay - stunned the boxing world when he captured the heavyweight title in Miami. Clay was declared the winner when Sonny Liston failed to answer the bell for the seventh round in their first meeting.

Trivia Answer: Michael Ray Richardson

FEBRUARY

Today's Trivia: On February 26, 1935, Babe Ruth signed with what MLB team after being released by the New York Yankees?

Birthdays: Grover Cleveland Alexander, 1887; Preacher Roe, 1916; Rolando Blackman, 1959; Kelly Gruber, 1962; J.T. Snow, 1968; Marshall Faulk, 1973; Mark DeRosa, 1975; Robert Mathis, 1981

On This Day: In 1998, holdout Sergei Fedorov agreed to a contract with the Detroit Red Wings that would pay him $28 million if the team reached the Eastern Conference finals. He cashed in on it and then some as the Red Wings won their second straight Stanley Cup, led by Fedorov's 10 goals in 22 playoff games.

Trivia Answer: Boston Braves

FEBRUARY

Today's Trivia: On February 27, 1989, what baseball player, who would become known for wearing a batting helmet in the field, underwent surgery to remove a brain aneurysm?

Birthdays: Gene Sarazen, 1902; Johnny Pesky, 1919; Raymond Berry, 1933; John Davidson, 1953; James Worthy, 1961; Matt Stairs, 1968; Duce Staley, 1975; Tony Gonzalez, 1976; Devin Harris, 1983; Anibal Sanchez, 1984; Denard Span, 1984; Yovani Gallardo, 1986

On This Day: In 1992, Tiger Woods became the youngest golfer to play in a PGA Tour event in over three decades. Woods was just two months past his 16th birthday when he teed off at the Los Angeles Open.

Trivia Answer: John Olerud

FEBRUARY 28

Today's Trivia: On February 28, 1959, the Chicago Cardinals traded what future Hall of Fame running back to the Rams for nine players?

Birthdays: Frank Malzone, 1930; Dean Smith, 1931; Mario Andretti, 1940; Bubba Smith, 1945; Brian Billick, 1954; Adrian Dantley, 1956; Ickey Woods, 1966; Eric Lindros, 1973; Aroldis Chapman, 1988

On This Day: In 1967, Wilt Chamberlain finally missed a shot - after 11 days and 35 straight field goals, a new NBA record. Another NBA record was set exactly 14 years later when Calvin Murphy missed a free throw after 78 successful attempts.

Trivia Answer: Ollie Matson

FEBRUARY 29

Today's Trivia: On February 29, 1980, what Hartford Whaler became the first player in NHL history to score 800 career goals?

Birthdays: Pepper Martin, 1904; Al Rosen, 1924; Henri Richard, 1936; Monte Kiffin , 1940; Bryce Paup, 1968; Terrence Long, 1976

On This Day: In 1972, Henry Aaron signed a new contract with the Braves, making him the first Major League player to earn $200,000 a year.

Trivia Answer: Gordie Howe

MARCH

1

Today's Trivia: On March 1, 1969, the Commerce Comet called it a career, retiring from Major League Baseball. Who is he?

Birthdays: Harry Caray, 1914; Pete Rozelle, 1926; Mike Rozier, 1961; Chris Webber, 1973; Stephen Davis, 1974; Trevor Cahill, 1988; Michael Conforto, 1993

On This Day: In 1988, Wayne Gretzky set a new NHL career record for assists in the Edmonton Oilers 5-3 win over Los Angeles. Gretzky tallied his 1,050th assist in less than nine seasons, breaking a mark that took Gordie Howe 26 years to establish.

Trivia Answer: Mickey Mantle

MARCH

2

Today's Trivia: On March 2, 1951, Ed Macauley took home MVP honors in the first-ever edition of what sporting event?

Birthdays: Mel Ott, 1909; Denny Crum, 1937; Ian Woosnam, 1958; Terry Steinbach, 1962; Ron Gant, 1965; Jay Gibbons, 1977; Henrik Lundqvist, 1982; Ben Roethlisberger, 1982; Glen Perkins, 1983; Reggie Bush, 1985; Malcolm Butler, 1990

On This Day: In 1962, 4,124 fans in Hershey, Pennsylvania, witnessed the greatest scoring feat in NBA history. Wilt Chamberlain made 36 field goals and 28 free throws to become the only pro player to score 100 points in a game as the Philadelphia Warriors outgunned the New York Knicks, 169-147.

Trivia Answer: NBA All-Star Game

MARCH

Today's Trivia: On March 3, 1984, who was elected to succeed Bowie Kuhn as Commissioner of Major League Baseball?

Birthdays: Willie Keeler, 1872; Julius Boros, 1920; Randy Gradishar, 1952; Jackie Joyner-Kersee, 1962; Herschel Walker, 1962; Brian Leetch, 1968; Scott Radinsky, 1968; Jorge Julio, 1979; Santonio Holmes, 1984

On This Day: In 1985, Bill Shoemaker rode Lord at War to victory in the Santa Anita Handicap and became the first jockey to win $100 million in purses.

Trivia Answer: Peter Ueberroth

MARCH

Today's Trivia: On March 4, 1995, who was stripped of his WBA heavyweight title after refusing to fight mandatory opponent Tony Tucker?

Birthdays: Knute Rockne, 1888; Dazzy Vance, 1891; "Badger Bob" Johnson, 1931; Kevin Johnson, 1966; Jay Gruden, 1967; Brian Hunter, 1968; Robert Smith, 1972; Landon Donovan, 1982; Sergio Romo, 1983; Draymond Green, 1990; Nick Castellanos, 1992

On This Day: In 1990, the college basketball world mourned the loss of Hank Gathers. The Loyola Marymount star, who had a known heart issue, collapsed on the court and died during a game. Gathers was the second player in NCAA Division I history to lead the nation in scoring and rebounding in the same season.

Trivia Answer: George Foreman

MARCH

Today's Trivia: On March 5, 1973, Yankees pitchers Fritz Peterson and Mike Kekich announced a very unique trade. What did they wind up swapping?

Birthdays: Del Crandall, 1930; Fred Williamson, 1937; Kent Tekulve, 1947; Mike Munchak, 1960; Scott Skiles, 1964; Michael Irvin, 1966; Paul Konerko, 1976; Wally Szczerbiak, 1977; Erik Bedard, 1979; Kyle Schwarber, 1993; Emmanuel Mudiay, 1996

On This Day: In 1984, Brigham Young quarterback Steve Young signed a $42 million contract with the Los Angeles Express of the USFL. Unfortunately, the league folded later that year. Fortunately, for Young, his contract was guaranteed.

Trivia Answer: Their wives

MARCH

Today's Trivia: On March 6, 2000, what long-time Boston Bruin was traded to the Colorado Avalanche, where he would become a Stanley Cup champion in his final NHL game in 2001?

Birthdays: Lefty Grove, 1900; Cookie Rojas, 1939; Willie Stargell, 1940; Dick Fosbury, 1947; Sleepy Floyd, 1960; Shaquille O'Neal, 1972; Michael Finley, 1973; Clint Barmes, 1979; Tim Howard, 1979; Jake Arrieta, 1986; Francisco Cervelli, 1986

On This Day: In 1976, Dorothy Hamill became the first American woman in eight years to win the World Figure Skating Championship. Hamill also claimed the gold medal at the Winter Olympics that year.

Trivia Answer: Ray Bourque

MARCH

Today's Trivia: On March 7, 2009, what
17-year-old Brazilian soccer star made his professional
debut for Santos?

Birthdays: Janet Guthrie, 1938; Franco Harris, 1950;
J.R. Richard, 1950; Jeff Burroughs, 1951; Lynn Swann, 1952;
Joe Carter, 1960; Ivan Lendl, 1960; Jeff Kent, 1968

On This Day: In 1970, Notre Dame guard Austin Carr scored
61 points in a 112-82 win over Ohio University. Carr's effort broke
the NCAA Tournament single-game scoring record set five years
earlier by Bill Bradley of Princeton.

Trivia Answer: Neymar

MARCH

Today's Trivia: On March 8, 1954, the Milwaukee
Hawks and Baltimore Bullets took part in an NBA first (and last).
What was it?

Birthdays: Pete Dawkins, 1938; Dick Allen, 1942; Jim Rice, 1953;
Buck Williams, 1960; Kenny Smith, 1965; Jason Elam, 1970;
Juan Encarnacion, 1976; Hines Ward, 1976; Marcia Newby, 1988

On This Day: In 1971, the "Fight of the Century" between
Joe Frazier and Muhammad Ali took place at Madison Square
Garden in New York. The unbeaten Frazier won in 15 rounds in a
unanimous decision, handing Ali the first defeat of his pro career.

Trivia Answer: A two-team doubleheader
(Each contest was reduced from 48 to 40 minutes. The Hawks won both games.)

MARCH 9

Today's Trivia: On March 9, 1995, Major League Baseball owners officially welcomed what two expansion teams to the league by a vote of 28-0?

Birthdays: Jackie Jensen, 1927; Bert Campaneris, 1942; Mark Dantonio, 1956; Terry Mulholland, 1963; Phil Housley, 1964; Benito Santiago, 1965; Aaron Boone, 1973; Radek Dvorak, 1977; Clint Dempsey, 1983; Daniel Hudson, 1987

On This Day: In 1968, Elvin Hayes dropped 49 points and grabbed 27 rebounds as his Houston Cougars took down Loyola in the first round of the NCAA Tournament. Though his team lost in the Final Four, Hayes set a tourney record with 97 total rebounds.

Trivia Answer: Tampa Bay Devil Rays and Arizona Diamondbacks

MARCH 10

Today's Trivia: On March 10, 2002, who became the first and only NBA player to reach the 15,000-assist mark?

Birthdays: Marques Haynes, 1926; Joe Bugel, 1940; Jim Valvano, 1946; Austin Carr, 1948; Steve Howe, 1958; Andre Waters, 1962; Rod Woodson, 1965; Mike Timlin, 1966; Matt Kenseth, 1972; Shannon Miller, 1977; Kwame Brown, 1982; Zach LaVine, 1995

On This Day: In 1963, a rookie second baseman by the name of Pete Rose made his debut for the Cincinnati Reds, doubling twice in an exhibition game against the Chicago White Sox.

Trivia Answer: John Stockton

MARCH

11

Today's Trivia: On March 11, 1991, what 17-year-old put an end to Steffi Graf's run of 186 consecutive weeks when she became the #1-ranked tennis player in the world?

Birthdays: Dock Ellis, 1945; Cesar Geronimo, 1948; Bobby Abreu, 1974; Becky Hammon, 1977; Michal Handzus, 1977; Elton Brand, 1979; Dan Uggla, 1980; Greg Olsen, 1985; Anthony Davis, 1993

On This Day: In 1986, the NFL adopted an instant replay system to review disputed calls following a vote by league owners. After abandoning the idea six years later, the system would return for the 1999 season.

Trivia Answer: Monica Seles

MARCH

12

Today's Trivia: On March 12, 1903, the New York Highlanders joined baseball's American League. They are now known as the...?

Birthdays: Eddie Sutton, 1936; Jchnny Rutherford, 1938; Alberto Juantorena, 1951; Dale Murphy, 1956; Darryl Strawberry, 1962; Steve Finley, 1965; Raul Mondesi, 1971; Isaiah Rider, 1971

On This Day: In 2011, the UConn Huskies won the Big East Men's Basketball Tournament as a #9 seed by defeating Louisville, 69-66. That, however, was just the beginning of their magical run. UConn earned a #3 seed in the NCAA Tournament, where they ran the table, beating Butler to claim the school's third national championship.

Trivia Answer: New York Yankees

MARCH

13

Today's Trivia: On March 13, 2000, the first NFL quarterback to throw for 5,000 yards in a season officially announced his retirement. Who?

Birthdays: Frank "Home Run" Baker, 1886; Andy Bean, 1953; Mariano Duncan, 1963; Will Clark, 1964; Trent Dilfer, 1972; Johan Santana, 1979; Caron Butler, 1980; Manny Banuelos, 1991; Tristan Thompson, 1991; Mikaela Shiffrin, 1995

On This Day: In 1954, Braves starting outfielder Bobby Thomson fractured his ankle during an exhibition game, opening a spot in the lineup for a 20-year-old rookie named Henry Aaron.

Trivia Answer: Dan Marino

MARCH

14

Today's Trivia: On March 14, 1997, President Bill Clinton underwent surgery to repair an injured knee that he suffered that morning outside the house of what golfer?

Birthdays: Don Haskins, 1930; Wes Unseld, 1946; Butch Wynegar, 1956; Kirby Puckett, 1960; Kevin Brown, 1965; Larry Johnson, 1969; Ron Dayne, 1978; Bobby Jenks, 1981; Stephen Curry, 1988; Anthony Bennett, 1993; Simone Biles, 1997

On This Day: In 1967, in preparation for their merger, the AFL and NFL held their first combined draft. The Baltimore Colts chose Michigan State defensive lineman Bubba Smith with the first pick.

Trivia Answer: Greg Norman

MARCH

Today's Trivia: On March 15, 2015, what team handled Arkansas, 78-63, to claim the SEC Men's Basketball Tournament title and enter the NCAA Tournament undefeated?

Birthdays: Punch Imlach, 1918; Norm Van Brocklin, 1926; Bobby Bonds, 1946; Harold Baines, 1959; Terry Cummings, 1961; Mike Tomlin, 1972; Kevin Youkilis, 1979; Jon Jay, 1985; Eric Decker, 1987; Trayce Thompson, 1991; Devonta Freeman, 1992; Jabari Parker, 1995

On This Day: In 1970, Bobby Orr of the Boston Bruins became the first NHL defenseman to score 100 points in a season. Four goals against Detroit put Orr over the century mark.

Trivia Answer: Kentucky (They would go on to lose to Wisconsin in the Final Four.)

MARCH

Today's Trivia: On March 16, 2008, Allen Iverson and Carmelo Anthony led the way as what team scored 168 points in regulation to beat the Seattle Sonics by 52?

Birthdays: Lloyd Waner, 1906; Bob Ley, 1955; Ozzie Newsome, 1956; Mel Gray, 1961; Rodney Peete, 1966; Todd Heap, 1980; Curtis Granderson, 1981; Brian Wilson, 1982; Stephen Drew, 1983; Blake Griffin, 1989; Joel Embiid, 1994

On This Day: In 1938, Temple beat Colorado, 60-36, to win the first National Invitation Tournament and the Collegiate Basketball Championship. The NCAA staged its own tourney the following year to crown the national champs.

Trivia Answer: Denver Nuggets

MARCH

17

Today's Trivia: On March 17, 1955, fans rioted in Montreal after what hockey player was suspended for the remainder of the regular season following an incident in which he hit a linesman during a game?

Birthdays: Bobby Jones, 1902; Sonny Werblin, 1910; Sammy Baugh, 1914; Cito Gaston, 1944; Chuck Muncie, 1953; Danny Ainge, 1959; Bill Mueller, 1971; Mia Hamm, 1972; Kyle Korver, 1981; Chris Davis, 1986; Emmanuel Sanders, 1987; Juan Lagares, 1989; Jean Segura, 1990; Katie Ledecky, 1997

On This Day: In 1886, *The Sporting News* published its first issue. Copies sold for five cents each. Now only digital, the final print issues were shipped out at the end of 2012.

Trivia Answer: Maurice Richard

MARCH

18

Today's Trivia: On March 18, 1985, what two Hall of Famers who were previously banned from baseball after taking public relations jobs with casinos were reinstated by MLB?

Birthdays: Mike Webster, 1952; Guy Carbonneau, 1960; Curt Warner, 1961; Keith Millard, 1962; Bonnie Blair, 1964; Andre Rison, 1967; Scott Podsednik, 1976; Zdeno Chara, 1977; Fernando Rodney, 1977; Cory Schneider, 1986

On This Day: In 1945, Maurice "The Rocket" Richard scored with less than three minutes to play in a game against the Boston Bruins. For Richard, it was his 50th goal of the season, a first in NHL history.

Trivia Answer: Mickey Mantle and Willie Mays

MARCH

19

Today's Trivia: On March 19, 1960, what team led
by future NBA Hall of Famers Jerry Lucas and John
Havlicek won the 1960 NCAA Tournament?

Birthdays: Jay Berwanger, 1914; Guy Lewis, 1922;
Richie Ashburn, 1927; Joe Kapp, 1938; Scott May, 1954;
Andy Reid, 1958; Ivan Calderon, 1962; Andre Miller, 1976;
Steve Gleason, 1977; Clayton Kershaw, 1988

On This Day: In 1966, Texas Western defeated top-ranked
Kentucky for the college basketball title. It marked the first time that
an all-black starting five won the NCAA championship. The historic
journey of Don Haskins' team would be depicted in the 2006 film
Glory Road.

Trivia Answer: Ohio State Buckeyes, over California

MARCH

20

Today's Trivia: On March 20, 1934, "Mildred"
pitched one inning of scoreless ball in an exhibition game
for the Philadelphia Athletics. She had previously won two
gold medals at the 1932 Olympics. She is…?

Birthdays: Cale Yarborough, 1939; Pat Riley, 1945;
Bobby Orr, 1948; Chris Hoiles, 1965; Mookie Blaylock, 1967;
Jamal Crawford, 1980

On This Day: In 1973, Roberto Clemente was elected to the
Baseball Hall of Fame. Clemente's induction came less than three
months after his death in a plane crash while delivering relief
supplies to earthquake victims in Nicaragua.

Trivia Answer: Babe Didrikson Zaharias

MARCH

Today's Trivia: On March 21, 1961, what infamous owner purchased the Cleveland Browns franchise for just under $4 million?

Birthdays: Tom Flores, 1937; Tommy Davis, 1939; Manny Sanguillen, 1944; Jay Hilgenberg, 1959; Shawon Dunston, 1963; Al Iafrate, 1966; Cristian Guzman, 1978; Ronaldinho, 1980; Adrian Peterson, 1985; Carlos Carrasco, 1987

On This Day: In 1953, Boston outlasted Syracuse, 111-105, in an NBA playoff game that stretched into four overtime periods. Bob Cousy scored 50 points, including 25 after regulation, as a total of 12 players fouled out of the contest.

Trivia Answer: Art Modell

MARCH

Today's Trivia: On March 22, 1991, Wayne Gretzky and Kings owner Bruce McNall paid over $450,000 at an auction for a rare baseball card of what player?

Birthdays: Don Chaney, 1946; Bob Costas, 1952; Glenallen Hill, 1965; Ramon Martinez, 1968; Russell Maryland, 1969; Shawn Bradley, 1972; Cory Lidle, 1972; Marcus Camby, 1974; Joey Porter, 1977; Tom Poti, 1977; Juan Uribe, 1979; Thomas Davis, 1983; J.J. Watt, 1989

On This Day: In 1969, Lew Alcindor was named MVP of the NCAA Championship Game for the third year in a row. The UCLA center led his Bruin teammates to a 92-72 win over Purdue by dumping in 37 points.

Trivia Answer: Honus Wagner

MARCH

Today's Trivia: On March 23, 1952, what
Blackhawks Hall of Famer scored three goals in 21
seconds during a 7-6 win over the Rangers?

Birthdays: Roger Bannister, 1929; Lee May, 1943;
George Scott, 1944; Ron Jaworski, 1951; Geno Auriemma, 1954;
Moses Malone, 1955; Jason Kidd, 1973; Mark Buehrle, 1979;
Brandon Marshall, 1984; Maurice Jones-Drew, 1985;
Dellin Betances, 1988; Gordon Hayward, 1990; Kyrie Irving, 1992

On This Day: In 1994, Wayne Gretzky scored the 802nd goal of
his illustrious NHL career, surpassing Gordie Howe. The milestone
came in a Kings' 6-3 loss to the Vancouver Canucks. The Great One
would finish up with a final tally of 894.

Trivia Answer: Bill Mosienko

MARCH

Today's Trivia: On March 24, 1973, who finished
the NBA season by becoming the first player ever to lead
the league in both points and assists per game in the same season?

Birthdays: George Sisler, 1893; Larry Wilson, 1938;
Jesus Alou, 1942; Pat Bradley, 1951; Garry Templeton, 1956;
Bruce Hurst, 1958; Wilson Alvarez, 1970; Peyton Manning, 1976;
Jose Valverde, 1978; Corey Hart, 1982; T.J. Ford, 1983;
Chris Bosh, 1984; Starlin Castro, 1990

On This Day: In 2013, Florida Gulf Coast University defeated
San Diego State, 81-71, winning a second game in the Men's NCAA
Tournament. In doing so, they became the first 15-seed ever to reach
the Sweet 16. Their run would come to an end, however, with a loss
to Florida in their next game.

Trivia Answer: Nate "Tiny" Archibald

MARCH

25

Today's Trivia: On March 25, 1958, Walker Smith, Jr. defeated Carmen Basilio to regain the middleweight championship and earn the fifth title of his career. By what name is he better known?

Birthdays: Howard Cosell, 1918; Avery Johnson, 1965; Tom Glavine, 1966; Travis Fryman, 1969; Dan Wilson, 1969; Sheryl Swoopes, 1971; Neal Cotts, 1980; Danica Patrick, 1982; Kyle Lowry, 1986

On This Day: In 1973, a season of futility finally ended for the Philadelphia 76ers. A loss to Detroit in the last game of the year gave the team a 9-73 record, the worst in NBA history.

Trivia Answer: Sugar Ray Robinson

MARCH

26

Today's Trivia: On March 26, 2005, what #1-seed overcame a 15-point deficit with just over four minutes remaining to stun #3 Arizona in overtime and reach the Final Four?

Birthdays: Harry Kalas, 1936; Braulio Baeza, 1940; Ann Meyers, 1955; Marcus Allen, 1960; Kevin Seitzer, 1962; John Stockton, 1962; Jose Vizcaino, 1968; Michael Peca, 1974; Von Miller, 1989

On This Day: In 1979, Michigan State defeated Indiana State, 75-64, to win the NCAA Tournament. The spotlight was on two players whose rivalry continued in the NBA: Magic Johnson and Larry Bird. Johnson outscored Bird, 24-19, as the Spartans stopped the Sycamores' 33-game winning streak.

Trivia Answer: Illinois (They would lose to UNC in the title game.)

MARCH

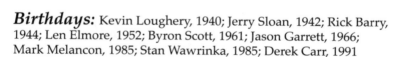

27

Today's Trivia: On March 27, 1994, Magic Johnson took over as head coach of the L.A. Lakers. His stint, however, would last just 16 games. His replacement would be named the 1994-95 NBA Coach of the Year. Who?

Birthdays: Miller Huggins, 1878; Cale Yarborough, 1939; Chris McCarron, 1955; Randall Cunningham, 1963; Michael Cuddyer, 1979; Buster Posey, 1987; Matt Harvey, 1989

On This Day: In 1939, Oregon took down Ohio State, 46–33, to win the first-ever NCAA Men's Basketball Tournament. Even in defeat, OSU's Jimmy Hull was named the tournament's Most Outstanding Player.

Trivia Answer: Del Harris

MARCH

28

Today's Trivia: On March 28, 1990, Michael Jordan dropped 69 vs. the same team he hit "The Shot" against in the previous year's playoffs. Who?

Birthdays: Kevin Loughery, 1940; Jerry Sloan, 1942; Rick Barry, 1944; Len Elmore, 1952; Byron Scott, 1961; Jason Garrett, 1966; Mark Melancon, 1985; Stan Wawrinka, 1985; Derek Carr, 1991

On This Day: In 1984, unannounced and in the middle of the night, moving vans loaded with Baltimore Colts equipment made their way out of town and headed for Indianapolis, where the Colts would make their new home.

Trivia Answer: Cleveland Cavaliers

MARCH

29

Today's Trivia: On March 29, 1987, what school, who currently trails only UConn in terms of titles, defeated Louisiana Tech to claim their first NCAA Women's Basketball Tournament championship?

Birthdays: Cy Young, 1867; Emlen Tunnell, 1925; Denny McLain, 1944; Walt Frazier, 1945; Earl Campbell, 1955; Billy Beane, 1962; Brian Jordan, 1967; Alex Ochoa, 1972; Jennifer Capriati, 1976; Justin Tuck, 1983

On This Day: In 1982, coach Dean Smith of North Carolina won his first NCAA tournament. The Tar Heels, led by freshman Michael Jordan, beat Georgetown and frosh center Patrick Ewing, 63-62.

Trivia Answer: Tennessee

MARCH

30

Today's Trivia: On March 30, 1987, what Hoosier hit the game-winner in the final seconds to give Indiana a 74-73 win over Syracuse for the national title?

Birthdays: Willie Galimore, 1935; Jerry Lucas, 1940; Bill Johnson, 1960; Lomas Brown, 1963; Secretariat, 1970; Richard Sherman, 1988; Chris Sale, 1989

On This Day: In 1993, the Ottawa Senators suffered their 37th consecutive road defeat at the hands of the Pittsburgh Penguins, 6-4. That equaled the NHL mark for road futility. After setting the record with another loss, the streak would stop at 38 with a win at the Islanders on April 10.

Trivia Answer: Keith Smart

MARCH

Today's Trivia: On March 31, 1998, what MLB team that was founded in 1969 played their first game as members of the National League?

Birthdays: Jack Johnson, 1878; Gordie Howe, 1928; Bob Pulford, 1936; Jimmy Johnson, 1938; Ed Marinaro, 1950; John Taylor, 1962; Tom Barrasso, 1965; Steve Smith, 1969; Pavel Bure, 1971; Chien-Ming Wang, 1980

On This Day: In 1931, a plane crash in Kansas claimed the life of Notre Dame football coach Knute Rockne at the age of 43. The Fighting Irish experienced several undefeated seasons and national championships during Rockne's 13-year tenure.

Trivia Answer: Milwaukee Brewers

APRIL

Today's Trivia: On April 1, 1985, what #8 seed shot nearly 80% from the field to shock #1 Georgetown, 66-64, and claim the NCAA men's title?

Birthdays: Bo Schembechler, 1929; Ron Perranoski, 1936; Phil Niekro, 1939; Rusty Staub, 1944; Norm Van Lier, 1947; Scott Stevens, 1964; Mark Jackson, 1965; Sean Taylor, 1983; Daniel Murphy, 1985; Brook & Robin Lopez, 1988

On This Day: In 1972, baseball players staged the first strike in the sport's history. The walkout was no April Fool's joke, lasting 13 days and disrupting the start of the new season.

Trivia Answer: Villanova

APRIL

Today's Trivia: On April 2, 1990, the UNLV
Runnin' Rebels became champions in men's hoops.
What school did they drop 103 points on in the title game
in a 30-point rout?

Birthdays: Luke Appling, 1907; Carmen Basilio, 1927;
Billy Pierce, 1927; Dick Radatz, 1937; Reggie Smith, 1945;
Don Sutton, 1945; Linford Christie, 1960; Pete Incaviglia, 1964;
Bill Romanowski, 1966; Jon Lieber, 1970

On This Day: In 1995, the Rebecca Lobo-led University
of Connecticut completed a perfect 35-0 season by upending
Tennessee, 70-64, for the NCAA National Women's Basketball
Championship.

Trivia Answer: Duke

APRIL

Today's Trivia: On April 3, 2012, what women's
basketball team became the first to go 40-0 in a single
season when they scored an 80-61 win over Notre Dame in
the title game?

Birthdays: Bernie Parent, 1945; Lyle Alzado, 1949;
Pervis Ellison, 1967; Rodney Hampton, 1969; Picabo Street, 1971;
Michael Olowokandi, 1975; Koji Uehara, 1975; Ryan Doumit, 1981;
Jared Allen, 1982; Jay Bruce, 1987; Jason Kipnis, 1987;
Kam Chancellor, 1988; Blake Swihart, 1992

On This Day: In 1989, Michigan beat Seton Hall, 80-79,
in overtime to win the NCAA Basketball Championship. The
Wolverines' Rumeal Robinson sank two free throws with three
seconds left to win it for Michigan. This nail-biter was the first
title game to go into OT in 26 years.

Trivia Answer: Baylor

APRIL

4

Today's Trivia: On April 4, 2016, Villanova defeated North Carolina in a championship game for the ages. Who hit the game-winning buzzer beater to give the Wildcats a 77-74 win?

Birthdays: Tris Speaker, 1888; Gil Hodges, 1924; JoAnne Carner, 1939; Jim Fregosi, 1942; Ray Fosse, 1947; John Hannah, 1951; Tom Jackson, 1951; Pat Burns, 1952; Andy MacPhail, 1953; Jack Del Rio, 1963; Dale Hawerchuk, 1963; Scott Rolen, 1975; Roberto Luongo, 1979; Ben Gordon, 1983; Frank Kaminsky, 1993

On This Day: In 1988, Toronto's George Bell became the first player in MLB history to hit three home runs on Opening Day. Exactly six years later, Tuffy Rhodes of the Cubs became the first National Leaguer to accomplish the feat.

Trivia Answer: Kris Jenkins

APRIL

5

Today's Trivia: On April 5, 2010, what future NBA player's half-court heave rimmed out at the buzzer as Duke survived to beat Butler, 61-59, for their fourth men's title?

Birthdays: Glenn "Pop" Warner, 1871; Ron Hansen, 1938; Doug Favell, 1945; Rennie Stennett, 1951; Brad Van Pelt, 1951; Marc Bulger, 1977; Stephen Jackson, 1978; Jorge De La Rosa, 1981

On This Day: In 1993, the Colorado Rockies and Florida Marlins each played their first games in franchise history. The Rockies lost to the Mets, 3-0, while the Marlins defeated the Dodgers, 6-3.

Trivia Answer: Gordon Hayward

APRIL

Today's Trivia: On April 6, 1896, the first modern Olympic Games began. Where were they held?

Birthdays: Mickey Cochrane, 1903; Ernie Lombardi, 1908; Spider Lockhart, 1943; Bert Blyleven, 1951; Sterling Sharpe, 1965; Tommy Greene, 1967; Bret Boone, 1969; Olaf Kolzig, 1970; Andy Phillips, 1977; Tim Hasselbeck, 1978

On This Day: In 1987, Sugar Ray Leonard became the middleweight champion of the world after a hotly disputed 12-round decision over Marvelous Marvin Hagler.

Trivia Answer: Athens, Greece

APRIL

Today's Trivia: On April 7, 1986, what Red Sox All-Star became the first player ever to hit the first pitch of Opening Day for a home run?

Birthdays: John McGraw, 1873; Bobby Doerr, 1918; Tony Dorsett, 1954; Buster Douglas, 1960; Ricky Watters, 1969; Brett Tomko, 1973; Ronde & Tiki Barber, 1975; Ronnie Belliard, 1975; Ben Petrick, 1977; Adrian Beltre, 1979; Danny Almonte, 1987

On This Day: In 2008, Kansas stunned Memphis in overtime, 75-68, to win the NCAA men's title. Up by nine with just over two minutes left in regulation, the Tigers missed several free throws and failed to close the door. The Jayhawks tied the game on a Mario Chalmers three-pointer with two seconds left. They ran away with it in the extra session.

Trivia Answer: Dwight Evans

APRIL

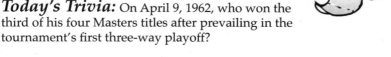

Today's Trivia: On April 8, 1975, who became the first full-time African-American manager in MLB history when he made his debut with the Cleveland Indians?

Birthdays: Sonja Henie, 1912; Charlie Maxwell, 1927; John Havlicek, 1940; Catfish Hunter, 1946; Gary Carter, 1954; Ricky Bell, 1955; Mark Clayton, 1961; Terry Porter, 1963; Alex Gonzalez, 1973; Shaka Smart, 1977; Jeremy Guthrie, 1979; Felix Hernandez, 1986; Carlos Santana, 1986; Jeremy Hellickson, 1987

On This Day: In 1974, Hank Aaron hit a 1-0 pitch off Al Downing into the left field bullpen for career home run #715, breaking the record held by Babe Ruth. Aaron clouted another 40 homers before retiring.

Trivia Answer: Frank Robinson

APRIL

Today's Trivia: On April 9, 1962, who won the third of his four Masters titles after prevailing in the tournament's first three-way playoff?

Birthdays: Curly Lambeau, 1898; Paul Arizin, 1928; Nate Colbert, 1946; Seve Ballesteros, 1957; Jose Guzman, 1963; Hal Morris, 1965; Graeme Lloyd, 1967; Jacques Villeneuve, 1971; David Robertson, 1985

On This Day: In 1978, the NBA regular season came to a close as San Antonio's George Gervin won the scoring title over Denver's David Thompson in historic fashion. After Thompson scored 73 points earlier in the day, Gervin poured in 63 in his season finale. Gervin's average jumped to 27.22 points per game, edging Thompson's 27.15.

Trivia Answer: Arnold Palmer

APRIL

10

Today's Trivia: On April 10, 1999, what team set an NBA record for the fewest points scored in a game in the shot clock era when they managed just 49 against the Heat?

Birthdays: John Madden, 1936; Don Meredith, 1938; Bob Watson, 1946; Mel Blount, 1948; Ken Griffey, 1950; Mike Devereaux, 1963; Neil Smith, 1966; Kasey Kahne, 1980; Andre Ethier, 1982; Corey Kluber, 1986; Chris Heston, 1988; Nerlens Noel, 1994

On This Day: In 2005, Tiger Woods won his fourth Masters title after hitting a 15-foot birdie on the first hole of a sudden-death playoff against Chris DiMarco.

Trivia Answer: Chicago Bulls (They lost, 82-49.)

APRIL

11

Today's Trivia: On April 11, 1990, Mark Langston pitched seven innings before Mike Witt hurled the final two frames as what team threw a combined no-hitter against the Mariners?

Birthdays: Michael Ray Richardson, 1955; Donnie Hammon, 1957; Bret Saberhagen, 1964; Jason Varitek, 1972; Trot Nixon, 1974; Kelvim Escobar, 1976; Mark Teixeira, 1980; Pete Kozma, 1988

On This Day: In 2004, Phil Mickelson claimed his first major championship by winning The Masters. Mickelson sunk an 18-foot birdie putt on the final hole to defeat Ernie Els by a single stroke. He would win his second Masters two years later.

Trivia Answer: California Angels

APRIL

Today's Trivia: On April 12, 2015, who won
The Masters by tying the 72-hole record set by Tiger Woods
and becoming the second-youngest winner, behind Woods?

Birthdays: Addie Joss, 1880; Joe Lapchick, 1900;
Johnny Antonelli, 1930; Mike Garrett, 1944; Lorenzo White, 1966;
Adam Graves, 1968; Paul Lo Duca, 1972; Hisashi Iwakuma, 1981

On This Day: In 1958, Bob Pettit scored 50 points to lead the
St. Louis Hawks to a 110-109 victory over the Boston Celtics and an
NBA championship. The win avenged the Hawks' loss to the Celtics
in the Finals the previous year.

Trivia Answer: Jordan Spieth

APRIL

Today's Trivia: On April 13, 2016, Stephen Curry
finished the regular season with a 46-point performance,
nailing 10 three-pointers in the process. In doing so, he
reached what milestone number for 3s in a season?

Birthdays: Bill Koch, 1943; Davis Love III, 1964;
Wes Chamberlain, 1966; Ted Washington, 1968; Bo Outlaw, 1971;
Patrik Elias, 1976; Baron Davis, 1979; Hunter Pence, 1983;
Lorenzo Cain, 1986; Josh Gordon, 1991

On This Day: In 2016, basketball fans were treated to two
doses of history. In his final NBA game, Kobe Bryant dropped 60
points in a 101-96 Lakers win over the Jazz. Meanwhile, the Golden
State Warriors won their 73rd game of the season, passing the
1995-96 Chicago Bulls in the record books with a blowout victory
over Memphis.

_Trivia Answer: 400 (The previous mark was 286, held by...Stephen Curry. He finished
with 402, to be exact.)_

APRIL

Today's Trivia: On April 14, 1910, who became the first U.S. President to throw out the ceremonial first pitch of the season at a Washington Senators-Philadelphia Athletics game?

Birthdays: Pete Rose, 1941; Cynthia Cooper, 1963; Stan Humphries, 1965; David Justice, 1966; Greg Maddux, 1966; Brad Ausmus, 1969; Steve Avery, 1970; Gregg Zaun, 1971; Kyle Farnsworth, 1976; Joe Haden, 1989

On This Day: In 1960, Montreal set an NHL record that has yet to be matched. Sweeping Toronto, 4-0, the Canadians captured their fifth Stanley Cup in a row.

Trivia Answer: William Howard Taft

APRIL

Today's Trivia: On April 15, 1997, Major League Baseball honored Jackie Robinson by retiring his jersey number throughout the league. What's the number?

Birthdays: Ed Bailey, 1931; Willie Davis, 1940; Michael Cooper, 1956; Evelyn Ashford, 1957; Dara Torres, 1967; Jeromy Burnitz, 1969; Jason Sehorn, 1971; Tim Thomas, 1974; Milton Bradley, 1978; Ilya Kovalchuk, 1983; Antonio Cromartie, 1984; John Danks, 1985; Chris Tillman, 1988

On This Day: In 1947, Jackie Robinson broke the color barrier that had excluded African-Americans from Major League Baseball. Playing first base for the Brooklyn Dodgers, Robinson went hitless in three at bats against the Boston Braves.

Trivia Answer: 42

APRIL

Today's Trivia: On April 16, 1940, what 21-year-old and future Hall of Famer threw the only Opening Day no-hitter in MLB history?

Birthdays: Paul Waner, 1903; Dick "Night Train" Lane, 1928; Jim Lonborg, 1942; Kareem Abdul-Jabbar, 1947; Bill Belichick, 1952; Bruce Bochy, 1955; Fernando Vina, 1969; Steve Emtman, 1970; Antonio Alfonseca, 1972; Luol Deng, 1985; Nolan Arenado, 1991

On This Day: In 1996, the Chicago Bulls became the first team in NBA history to win 70 games in a single regular season with an 86-80 win over the Bucks. They would finish 72-10 en route to their first of three consecutive titles. Exactly seven years later, Michael Jordan would play in his final NBA game, scoring 15 points in a Wizards loss to the 76ers.

Trivia Answer: Cleveland's Bob Feller, vs. the White Sox

APRIL

Today's Trivia: On April 17, 2012, who became the oldest pitcher in MLB history to win a game?

Birthdays: Alexander Cartwright, 1820; Cap Anson, 1852; Geoff Petrie, 1948; Borje Salming, 1951; Boomer Esiason, 1961; Ken Daneyko, 1964; Marquis Grissom, 1967; Theo Ratliff, 1973; Jed Lowrie, 1984

On This Day: In 1976, Mike Schmidt's four consecutive home runs turned a 13-2 Cubs lead into an 18-16 Phillies win. The last of Schmidt's homers was the game-winner in the 10th inning.

Trivia Answer: Jamie Moyer, at just under 49 ½ years old, with the Rockies

APRIL

Today's Trivia: On April 18, 1999, Wayne Gretzky played in his final NHL game as what team fell in overtime to the Pittsburgh Penguins?

Birthdays: Richie Petitbon, 1938; Pete Gogolak, 1942; Jim Eisenreich, 1959; Wilbur Marshall, 1962; Willie Roaf, 1970; Derrick Brooks, 1973; Miguel Cabrera, 1983; Billy Butler, 1986; Henderson Alvarez, 1990

On This Day: In 1923, Babe Ruth christened the "House That Ruth Built" with a three-run home run. A crowd of 74,200 attended the first game ever played in Yankee Stadium, a 4-1 triumph over the Red Sox.

Trivia Answer: New York Rangers

APRIL

Today's Trivia: On April 19, 1997, what future Hall of Famer was selected #1 overall by the St. Louis Rams in the NFL Draft?

Birthdays: Bucky Walters, 1909; Jack Pardee, 1936; Alexis Arguello, 1952; Frank Viola, 1960; Spike Owen, 1961; Al Unser, Jr., 1962; Keith Jackson, 1965; Jose Cruz, Jr., 1974; Troy Polamalu, 1981; Zach Duke, 1983; Joe Mauer, 1983; Candace Parker, 1986; Maria Sharapova, 1987; Jackie Bradley, Jr., 1990

On This Day: In 1897, 15 runners competed in the first Boston Marathon. New Yorker John J. McDermott crossed the finish line in 2:55:10 to win the race. Five of the competitors dropped out.

Trivia Answer: Orlando Pace

APRIL

Today's Trivia: On April 20, 1916, Weeghman
Park held its first National League baseball game.
By what "friendly" name is the stadium now known?

Birthdays: Ernie Stautner, 1925; Harry Agganis, 1929;
Steve Spurrier, 1945; Don Mattingly, 1961; Allan Houston, 1971;
Todd Hollandsworth, 1973; Danny Granger, 1983; Brent Seabrook,
1985; Brandon Belt, 1988; Luke Kuechly, 1991

On This Day: In 1986, Michael Jordan set a postseason record
with a 63-point showing against the Boston Celtics. Despite Jordan's
efforts, the Bulls fell to the Celtics in double overtime, 135-131.
Boston would go on to sweep Chicago in three games and later
defeat Houston for the NBA title.

Trivia Answer: Wrigley Field, home to the Chicago Cubs

APRIL

Today's Trivia: On April 21, 2012, what White Sox
pitcher threw the 21st perfect game in MLB history in
what was also the first complete game of his big league career?

Birthdays: Steve Owens, 1898; Gary Peters, 1937;
Al Bumbry, 1947; Jesse Orosco, 1957; Ken Caminiti, 1963;
Ed Belfour, 1965; Tony Romo, 1980; Joc Pederson, 1992

On This Day: In 1980, Bill Rodgers won the Boston
Marathon for the third consecutive time. The women's winner
was a controversial one as Rosie Ruiz crossed the finish line first
but was disqualified for not running the entire course. Jacqueline
Gareau of Canada was declared the winner.

Trivia Answer: Philip Humber

APRIL

Today's Trivia: On April 22, 2010, what team destroyed the Pirates, 20-0, capping off a three-game sweep in which they outscored Pittsburgh 36-1?

Birthdays: Spencer Haywood, 1949; Terry Francona, 1959; Freeman McNeil, 1959; Jeff Hostetler, 1961; Jimmy Key, 1961; Mickey Morandini, 1966; Marshawn Lynch, 1986; Tyson Ross, 1987; Dee Gordon, 1988

On This Day: In 2004, former Cardinals safety Pat Tillman lost his life while serving his country in Afghanistan. Tillman, a College Football Hall of Famer, turned down a multi-million dollar contract from Arizona to enlist in the U.S. Army in 2002.

Trivia Answer: Milwaukee Brewers

APRIL

Today's Trivia: On April 23, 1950, the Lakers won their first NBA title by beating the Syracuse Nationals, four games to two. What city did the champs call home at the time?

Birthdays: Jim Bottomley, 1900; Bud Wilkinson, 1916; Warren Spahn, 1921; Tony Esposito, 1943; Gail Goodrich, 1943; Claude Julien, 1960; Sam Madison, 1974; Andruw Jones, 1977

On This Day: In 1939, Ted Williams hit the first home run of his Major League career. Exactly 15 years later, Hammerin' Hank Aaron connected on his first MLB homer.

Trivia Answer: Minneapolis

APRIL

Today's Trivia: On April 24, 2004, what team selected an unhappy Eli Manning first overall in the NFL Draft before dealing him to the New York Giants?

Birthdays: Carroll Dale, 1938; Bill Singer, 1944; Vince Ferragamo, 1954; Mike Blowers, 1965; Omar Vizquel, 1967; Todd Jones, 1968; Chipper Jones, 1972; Eric Snow, 1973; Carlos Beltran, 1977; Kris Letang, 1987

On This Day: In 1967, the Philadelphia 76ers beat the San Francisco Warriors, 125-122, to capture the NBA title in six games. It marked the first time in nine years that the Boston Celtics had not won the championship.

Trivia Answer: San Diego Chargers

APRIL

Today's Trivia: On April 25, 1964, what team, who hasn't won a title since 1967, defeated the Detroit Red Wings to claim a third consecutive Stanley Cup?

Birthdays: Meadowlark Lemon, 1932; Bob Gutowski, 1935; Vladislav Tretiak, 1952; Randy Cross, 1954; Tony Phillips, 1959; Adam Silver, 1962; Joe Buck, 1969; Travis Fryman, 1969; Darren Woodson, 1969; Jacque Jones, 1975; Tim Duncan, 1976; DeAngelo Williams, 1983

On This Day: In 1976, Chicago outfielder Rick Monday stepped in to save the American flag after two war protesters ran onto the field during a game at Dodger Stadium with the intention of burning it. Monday would later receive a Bicentennial Commendation from President Gerald Ford.

Trivia Answer: Toronto Maple Leafs

APRIL

26

Today's Trivia: On April 26, 2012, the Colts selected Andrew Luck in the NFL Draft. On April 26, 1983, they took another quarterback #1 overall. Who was it?

Birthdays: Hack Wilson, 1900; Sal Maglie, 1917; Harry Gallatin, 1927; Donna de Varona, 1947; Amos Otis, 1947; Mike Scott, 1955; Natrone Means, 1972; Craig Adams, 1977; Kosuke Fukudome, 1977; Joe Crede, 1978

On This Day: In 1931, Lou Gehrig was called out for passing a runner after hitting a home run. It would prove costly, as he would go on to share the AL home run title with Babe Ruth with 46. Exactly 30 years later, Roger Maris hit his first homer of the year. He would hit 60 more to break Ruth's single-season record set in 1927.

Trivia Answer: John Elway, who was traded to the Broncos

APRIL

27

Today's Trivia: On April 27, 1996, who became part of the only father/son combo in the 300-300 club (home runs and steals) when he hit homer #300 against the Marlins?

Birthdays: Rogers Hornsby, 1896; Enos Slaughter, 1916; Chuck Knox, 1932; Earl Anthony, 1938; Lee Roy Jordan, 1941; George Gervin, 1952; Herman Edwards, 1954; Chris Carpenter, 1975; Pedro Feliz, 1975; Keenan Allen, 1992; Corey Seager, 1994

On This Day: In 1956, Rocky Marciano announced his retirement from boxing at the age of 32. Marciano remains the only man to retire as heavyweight champ with a perfect record, having won all 49 of his fights.

Trivia Answer: Barry Bonds (father Bobby Bonds)

APRIL

28

Today's Trivia: On April 28, 1967, Muhammad Ali was stripped of his heavyweight title, but not because he lost a fight. What happened?

Birthdays: Tom Browning, 1960; Mark Bavaro, 1963; Barry Larkin, 1964; John Daly, 1966; Nicklas Lidstrom, 1970; Josh Howard, 1980; Chris Kaman, 1982; David Freese, 1983; Dillon Gee, 1986; Blake Bortles, 1992

On This Day: In 1966, the Boston Celtics won their eighth consecutive NBA title, beating the Los Angeles Lakers in Game 7, 95-93. Celtics coach Red Auerbach resigned after the game to become the team's general manager.

Trivia Answer: He refused to be drafted into the U.S. Army, citing religious reasons.

APRIL

29

Today's Trivia: On April 29, 1970, Mr. Clutch sank a 60-foot shot to send Game 3 of the NBA Finals vs. the Knicks into overtime. Who is he?

Birthdays: George Allen, 1918; Luis Aparicio, 1934; Johnny Miller, 1947; Jim Ryun, 1947; Rick Burleson, 1951; Dale Earnhardt, 1951; Ron Washington, 1952; Mike Babcock, 1963; John Vander Wal, 1966; Andre Agassi, 1970; Tony Armas, 1978; Jay Cutler, 1983; David Lee, 1983; Jonathan Toews, 1988

On This Day: In 1986, Roger Clemens established a new Major League record for strikeouts in a nine-inning game. The Bosox right-hander whiffed 20 batters, including eight in a row, in a win over the Seattle Mariners. Clemens would later match his own mark in a 1996 game against the Tigers.

Trivia Answer: Jerry West (The Lakers would lose the game, and ultimately, the series.)

APRIL

30

Today's Trivia: On April 30, 1971, what team claimed its lone NBA championship to date by sweeping the Baltimore Bullets?

Birthdays: Don Schollander, 1946; Phil Garner, 1949; Isiah Thomas, 1961; Al Toon, 1963; Michael Waltrip, 1963; Dave Meggett, 1966; Luis Scola, 1980

On This Day: In 1939, Lou Gehrig played in his 2,130th consecutive game, the last in his career. Amyotrophic lateral sclerosis not only brought an end to the Yankee great's streak, but also claimed his life two years later.

Trivia Answer: Milwaukee Bucks

MAY

1

Today's Trivia: On May 1, 1991, Rickey Henderson passed what Hall of Famer to become MLB's all-time leader in stolen bases with 939?

Birthdays: Chuck Bednarik, 1925; Ollie Matson, 1930; Eddie Johnson, 1959; Steve Cauthen, 1960; Gary Clark, 1962; Curtis Martin, 1973; Wes Welker, 1981

On This Day: In 1991, 44-year-old Nolan Ryan threw the seventh and final no-hitter of his career. Ryan fanned 16 as he shut down Toronto, 3-0. He remains the all-time leader in no-nos.

Trivia Answer: Lou Brock

MAY

Today's Trivia: On May 2, 2015, it was Floyd Mayweather, Jr. vs. Manny Pacquiao in one of the most-hyped bouts of all-time. What was the result of the fight?

Birthdays: Eddie Collins, 1887; Clay Carroll, 1941; Jamaal Wilkes, 1953; Russ Grimm, 1959; David Beckham, 1975; Sarah Hughes, 1985; Kyle Busch, 1985; Jarrod Saltalamacchia, 1985; Neftali Feliz, 1988; Paul George, 1990

On This Day: In 2002, Mariners outfielder Mike Cameron became the 13th major leaguer to hit four homers in one game in a 15-4 win over the White Sox. The first two dingers followed homers by second baseman Bret Boone, making it the first time the same two teammates hit back-to-back homers twice in one inning.

Trivia Answer: After 12 rounds, Mayweather won by a unanimous decision.

MAY

Today's Trivia: On May 3, 1981, what team completed its playoff collapse by losing the Eastern Conference Finals to the Celtics after being up three games to one and blowing double-digit leads in each of the final three contests?

Birthdays: Red Ruffing, 1905; Sugar Ray Robinson, 1921; Davey Lopes, 1945; Greg Gumbel, 1946; Gar Heard, 1948; Rod Langway, 1957; Jeff Hornacek, 1963; Ron Hextall, 1964; Ryan Dempster, 1977; Joseph Addai, 1983; Homer Bailey, 1986; Ben Revere, 1988

On This Day: In 1952, Eddie Arcaro rode Hill Gail to victory in the Kentucky Derby. Arcaro also rode into the record books, becoming the first jockey to win the "Run for the Roses" five times. Exactly 34 years later, 54-year-old Bill Shoemaker, aboard Ferdinand, became the oldest jockey to win the Derby.

Trivia Answer: Philadelphia 76ers

MAY

4

Today's Trivia: On May 4, 1994, who scored 56 of his team's 140 points to help finish off a three-game sweep of the Warriors in the NBA Playoffs?

Birthdays: Elmer Layden, 1903; Betsy Rawls, 1928; Rick Leach, 1957; Rohn Stark, 1959; Dawn Staley, 1970; Ben Grieve, 1976; Erin Andrews, 1978; James Harrison, 1978; Rory McIlroy, 1989; Victor Oladipo, 1992

On This Day: In 1957, Bill Shoemaker, the jockey of Gallant Man, misjudged the finish line at Churchill Downs, allowing Iron Liege to pass him and take the Kentucky Derby. Inexplicably, Shoemaker stood up in the stirrups to prematurely celebrate. His horse would lose in a photo finish.

Trivia Answer: Charles Barkley, with the Suns

MAY

5

Today's Trivia: On May 5, 1904, baseball's all-time leader in wins (and losses) by a pitcher threw the first perfect game of the modern era. Who is he?

Birthdays: Tony Canadeo, 1919; Bob Cerv, 1925; Larry Hisle, 1947; Steve Scott, 1956; Charles Nagy, 1967; Hideki Irabu, 1969; LaPhonso Ellis, 1970; Harold Miner, 1971; Muhsin Muhammad, 1973; Ike Taylor, 1980

On This Day: In 1969, the frustration continued for the Los Angeles Lakers. For the seventh time in 11 years, the Lakers lost the NBA Championship Series to the Celtics. Boston won Game 7, 108-106, despite 42 points and a triple double from Lakers guard Jerry West.

Trivia Answer: Cy Young

MAY

6

Today's Trivia: On May 6, 2000, Indiana defeated
Philadelphia in an NBA postseason contest as what two
Pacers made history by each dropping 40 points?

Birthdays: Weeb Ewbank, 1907; Willie Mays, 1931;
Rubin "Hurricane" Carter, 1937; Martin Brodeur, 1972;
John Abraham, 1978; Jason Witten, 1982; Chris Paul, 1985;
Goran Dragic, 1986; Gerardo Parra, 1987; Jose Altuve, 1990

On This Day: In 1954, Roger Bannister became the first man to
run the mile in less than four minutes. The British student broke the
tape in 3:59.4.

Trivia Answer: Jalen Rose and Reggie Miller

MAY

7

Today's Trivia: On May 7, 1994, what NBA team
became the first #8 seed to beat a #1 in a playoff series by
taking out Seattle with a thrilling Game 5 OT win?

Birthdays: Dick Williams, 1929; Babe Parilli, 1930;
Johnny Unitas, 1933; Louis Orr, 1958; Shawn Marion, 1978;
James Loney, 1984; Alex Smith, 1984; Earl Thomas, 1989

On This Day: In 1972, after losing in their previous eight NBA
Finals appearances, the Lakers finally won it all. Los Angeles beat
the New York Knicks, 114-100, to take the series, four games to one.
The Lakers' historic 69-win regular season had included a record
33-game winning streak.

Trivia Answer: Denver Nuggets

MAY

Today's Trivia: On May 8, 1968, what A's pitcher hurled the first regular season perfect game in the American League in nearly 50 years?

Birthdays: Francis Ouimet, 1893; Sonny Liston, 1932; Mike Cuellar, 1937; Mike D'Antoni, 1951; Bill Cowher, 1957; Lovie Smith, 1958; Ronnie Lott, 1959; Bobby Labonte, 1964; Felix Jose, 1965; Korey Stringer, 1974; John Maine, 1981; Alfredo Simon, 1981; Adrian Gonzalez, 1982; Kemba Walker, 1990

On This Day: In 1970, Willis Reed limped out of the locker room and onto the court as the Knicks won the NBA title over the Lakers with a 113-99 Game 7 triumph. While Reed was named the MVP, Walt Frazier stole the show in the clincher with 36 points and 19 assists.

Trivia Answer: Catfish Hunter

MAY

Today's Trivia: On May 9, 1984, Harold Baines hit a walk-off homer as what team defeated the Brewers in a 25 inning, 8 hour marathon that began the previous day and was suspended after the first 17 innings?

Birthdays: Pancho Gonzales, 1928; Ralph Boston, 1939; Calvin Murphy, 1948; Tony Gwynn, 1960; Steve Yzerman, 1965; Aaron Harang, 1978; Brandon Webb, 1979; Prince Fielder, 1984; Chase Headley, 1984; Jake Long, 1985

On This Day: In 1961, Baltimore Orioles first baseman Jim Gentile set a Major League record, hitting grand slam homers in consecutive at bats. Gentile supplied eight of the runs in Baltimore's 13-5 beating of Minnesota. (In 1999, Fernando Tatis one-upped Gentile, hitting two grand slams in one inning!)

Trivia Answer: Chicago White Sox

MAY

10

Today's Trivia: On May 10, 1987, what Warriors guard set playoff records for points in a quarter (29) and a half (39) to lead his team to an upset over the eventual NBA champion Lakers?

Birthdays: Pat Summerall, 1930; Tamara Press, 1937; Jim Calhoun, 1942; Jim Zorn, 1953; Chris Berman, 1955; Phil & Steve Mahre, 1957; Robby Thompson, 1962; Rony Seikaly, 1965; Salvador Perez, 1990; Missy Franklin, 1995

On This Day: In 1970, Bobby Orr's iconic overtime goal gave the Boston Bruins a 4-3 win and a sweep of the St. Louis Blues in the Stanley Cup Finals. It was the first NHL championship in 29 years for the Bruins.

Trivia Answer: Sleepy Floyd (He finished the game with 51.)

MAY

11

Today's Trivia: On May 11, 1971, Cleveland pitcher Steve Dunning hit a grand slam against Oakland. It remained the last grand slam hit by an American League pitcher until what Mariner matched the feat in 2008?

Birthdays: Charlie Gehringer, 1903; Rip Sewell, 1907; Jack Twyman, 1934; Milt Pappas, 1939; Bobby Witt, 1964; Francisco Cordero, 1975; Lauren Jackson, 1981; Matt Leinart, 1983; Jeremy Maclin, 1988; Brad Marchand, 1988; Cam Newton, 1989; Miguel Sano, 1993

On This Day: In 1972, the San Francisco Giants traded 41-year-old Willie Mays to the New York Mets in exchange for pitcher Charlie Williams and $50,000. The baseball legend would spend his final two seasons with the Mets, where he became the oldest position player to appear in a World Series game in 1973.

Trivia Answer: Felix Hernandez

MAY

Today's Trivia: On May 12, 1977, Joe Namath signed a deal with what team for his final season in the NFL?

Birthdays: Yogi Berra, 1925; Felipe Alou, 1935; Johnny Bucyk, 1935; George Karl, 1951; Lou Whitaker, 1957; Kevin Bass, 1959; Tony Hawk, 1968; Jim Furyk, 1970; Lawrence Phillips, 1975; Chris Hovan, 1978; Steve Smith, 1979; Lance Lynn, 1987

On This Day: In 1985, the NBA held its first Draft Lottery. Conspiracy theories arose when the New York Knicks, who finished the season with the league's third-worst record, won the right to the first pick. They would use it on Georgetown big man Patrick Ewing the following month.

Trivia Answer: Los Angeles Rams

MAY

Today's Trivia: On May 13, 1973, who did Bobby Riggs defeat in the original "Battle of the Sexes"?

Birthdays: Joe Louis, 1914; Bobby Valentine, 1950; Dennis Rodman, 1961; Jose Rijo, 1965; Mike Bibby, 1978; Barry Zito, 1978; Tyrann Mathieu, 1992

On This Day: In 1976, the New York Nets defeated the Denver Nuggets, 112-106, to win the American Basketball Association title in six games. It was the last hurrah for the ABA, which saw four of its teams absorbed by the NBA for the 1976-77 season.

Trivia Answer: Margaret Court

MAY

Today's Trivia: On May 14, 1981, the Celtics won the NBA title in six games by defeating what team that posted a 40-42 record during the regular season?

Birthdays: Earle Combs, 1899; Dick Howser, 1936; Tony Perez, 1942; Dave LaRoche, 1948; Dennis Martinez, 1955; Pat Borders, 1963; Joey Cora, 1965; Tony Siragusa, 1967; Roy Halladay, 1977; Frank Gore, 1983; Clay Matthews, 1986; Christian Colon, 1989; Rob Gronkowski, 1989

On This Day: In 1967, Mickey Mantle hit career home run #500 off of Baltimore's Stu Miller. He'd finish his career with 536. Exactly 19 years later, Reggie Jackson would pass The Mick when he hit #537 off of Roger Clemens.

Trivia Answer: Houston Rockets

MAY

Today's Trivia: On May 15, 1984, what NBA franchise announced that it was moving from San Diego to another California location?

Birthdays: Don Nelson, 1940; George Brett, 1953; Dan Patrick, 1956; John Smoltz, 1967; Emmitt Smith, 1969; Desmond Howard, 1970; Rod Smith, 1970; Ray Lewis, 1975; Josh Beckett, 1980; Justin Morneau, 1981; Michael Brantley, 1987; Brian Dozier, 1987; Andy Murray, 1987

On This Day: In 1973, Nolan Ryan threw the first of his seven career no-hitters as the California Angels shut down Kansas City, 3-0. Exactly eight years later, Cleveland's Len Barker would pitch the tenth perfect game in MLB history.

Trivia Answer: The Clippers, to Los Angeles

MAY

Today's Trivia: On May 16, 1999, #8-seeded New York upset #1 Miami in the NBA Playoffs when what Knick hit the game-winner with .8 seconds left to give his team a one-point victory in the deciding Game 5?

Birthdays: Billy Martin, 1928; Rick Reuschel, 1949; Rick Rhoden, 1953; Olga Korbut, 1955; Jack Morris, 1955; Joan Benoit Samuelson, 1957; Thurman Thomas, 1966; Gabriela Sabatini, 1970; Jean-Sebastien Giguere, 1977; Corey Perry, 1985

On This Day: In 1980, rookie Magic Johnson willed his Lakers to the NBA title with a performance for the ages. Filling in at center for the injured Kareem Abdul-Jabbar, Magic scored 42 points and grabbed 15 rebounds, leading L.A. to a 123-107 Game 6 win over Philadelphia.

Trivia Answer: Allan Houston

MAY

Today's Trivia: On May 17, 1983, what team completed a four-game sweep of the Oilers to claim their fourth consecutive Stanley Cup title?

Birthdays: James "Cool Papa" Bell, 1903; Earl Morrall, 1934; Norv Turner, 1952; Sugar Ray Leonard, 1956; Pascual Perez, 1957; Jim Nantz, 1959; Danny Manning, 1966; Jose Guillen, 1976; Carlos Pena, 1978; Tony Parker, 1982; Matt Ryan, 1985

On This Day: In 1998, David Wells pitched a perfect game for the Yankees in a 4-0 win over the Minnesota Twins. Coincidentally, Wells went to the same high school as Don Larsen, who pitched a perfect game for New York in the 1956 World Series.

Trivia Answer: New York Islanders

MAY

18

Today's Trivia: On May 18, 1998, Michael Jordan was named the NBA MVP for the fifth time in his career. With six, who is the only player to have more?

Birthdays: Fred Perry, 1909; Brooks Robinson, 1937; Reggie Jackson, 1946; Jari Kurri, 1960; Eric Young, 1967; Flozell Adams, 1975; Marcus Giles, 1978; Vince Young, 1983; Joakim Soria, 1984; Robert Quinn, 1990

On This Day: In 1995, two months after Michael Jordan made his return to basketball, his Bulls were eliminated from the playoffs in the second round by the Orlando Magic. It would be the last time a Bulls team led by MJ would lose in the postseason, as Chicago claimed the NBA title the next three seasons.

Trivia Answer: Kareem Abdul-Jabbar

MAY

19

Today's Trivia: On May 19, 2008, who caught his MLB record fourth no-hitter when he was behind the plate for Jon Lester's gem against the Royals?

Birthdays: Gil McDougald, 1928; Dolph Schayes, 1928; Bill Fitch, 1934; Archie Manning, 1949; Rick Cerone, 1954; Bill Laimbeer, 1957; Turk Wendell, 1967; London Fletcher, 1975; Kevin Garnett, 1976; Brandon Inge, 1977

On This Day: In 1974, goalie Bernie Parent led Philadelphia to 1-0 victory over Boston to give the Flyers their first Stanley Cup. The Flyers had entered the NHL as an expansion team just seven years earlier. Exactly 10 years later, the Oilers would begin their dynasty by beating the Islanders to claim their first of five Cups in seven seasons.

Trivia Answer: Jason Varitek, with the Red Sox

MAY 20

Today's Trivia: On May 20, 1995, whose Game 7 "Kiss of Death" three-pointer with seconds remaining lifted the eventual NBA champion Rockets over the Suns and into the Conference Finals?

Birthdays: Hal Newhouser, 1921; Bud Grant, 1927; Ken Boyer, 1931; Stan Mikita, 1940; Sadaharu Oh, 1940; Leroy Kelly, 1942; Bobby Murcer, 1946; David Wells, 1963; Todd Stottlemyre, 1965; Terrell Brandon, 1970; Ramon Hernandez, 1976; Jayson Werth, 1979; Austin Kearns, 1980

On This Day: In 1919, Babe Ruth hit his first career grand slam while also getting the win as Boston's starting pitcher. Exactly 80 years later, Robin Ventura became the first player to hit a grand slam in each game of a doubleheader as his Mets beat the Brewers twice.

Trivia Answer: Mario Elie

MAY 21

Today's Trivia: On May 21, 1977, what horse beat Iron Constitution by a length and a half to take the Preakness Stakes before winning the Triple Crown three weeks later?

Birthdays: Earl Averill, 1902; Ara Parseghian, 1923; Johnny Majors, 1935; Bobby Cox, 1941; Dave Wannstedt, 1952; Kent Hrbek, 1960; Dorsey Levens, 1970; Ricky Williams, 1977; Josh Hamilton, 1981; Matt Wieters, 1986

On This Day: In 1986, Ralph Sampson sent the Rockets to the NBA Finals with a buzzer beater that knocked out the Lakers and gave Houston a 4-1 series win. With just one second left and the score tied at 112, Sampson caught an inbounds pass and threw up an off-balance shot that went in. The Rockets would lose to Boston in the title round.

Trivia Answer: Seattle Slew

MAY

22

Today's Trivia: On May 22, 2003, who became the first female in nearly 60 years to play on the PGA Tour when she took part in the Bank of America Colonial Tournament?

Birthdays: Al Simmons, 1902; Mick Tingelhoff, 1940; Tommy John, 1943; David Blatt, 1959; Mike Breen, 1961; Jose Mesa, 1966; Julian Tavarez, 1973; Apolo Anton Ohno, 1982; Julian Edelman, 1986; Eric Sogard, 1986; Novak Djokovic, 1987

On This Day: In 1977, Janet Guthrie became the first woman to qualify for the Indianapolis 500. Her first Indy 500 would end after only 27 laps when mechanical problems forced her car out of the race.

Trivia Answer: Annika Sorenstam

MAY

23

Today's Trivia: On May 23, 1941, what "Brown Bomber" retained his heavyweight title by defeating Buddy Baer?

Birthdays: Rod Thorn, 1941; John Newcombe, 1944; Anatoly Karpov, 1951; Marvelous Marvin Hagler, 1954; Buck Showalter, 1956; James Hasty, 1965; Victor Espinoza, 1972; Charles Rogers, 1981; Jordan Zimmermann, 1986; Aaron Donald, 1991

On This Day: In 1922, boxer Gene Tunney suffered the only defeat of his career. Tunney lost by decision to Harry Greb in a light-heavyweight championship bout. Tunney avenged the defeat before moving up to heavyweight and winning that crown.

Trivia Answer: Joe Louis

MAY

24

Today's Trivia: On May 24, 1988, a power outage at what venue resulted in Game 4 of the Stanley Cup Finals between the Oilers and Bruins being cancelled?

Birthdays: Jim Mora, 1935; Mitch Kupchak, 1954; Joe Dumars, 1963; Pat Verbeek, 1964; Danny Bautista, 1972; Bartolo Colon, 1973; Brad Penny, 1978; Tracy McGrady, 1979; Joey Logano, 1990

On This Day: In 1935, President Franklin Delano Roosevelt pressed a button at the White House that turned on the lights for Major League Baseball's first night game. More than 20,000 fans watched at Crosley Field in Cincinnati as the Reds beat the Phillies, 2-1.

Trivia Answer: Boston Garden (The game was 3-3 when it was abandoned. Edmonton would win Game "5", sweeping the series 4-0.)

MAY

25

Today's Trivia: On May 25, 1935, what Ohio State and Olympic legend set three track and field world records and tied another at a Big Ten meet in Ann Arbor, Michigan?

Birthdays: Gene Tunney, 1898; Lindsey Nelson, 1919; Bill Sharman, 1926; K.C. Jones, 1932; John Montefusco, 1950; Dave Hollins, 1966; Kendall Gill, 1968; Todd Walker, 1973; Miguel Tejada, 1974; Brian Urlacher, 1978; Chris Young, 1979; Jason Kubel, 1982; Shawne Merriman, 1984

On This Day: In 1965, Muhammad Ali (nee Cassius Clay) knocked out Sonny Liston in the first round of their championship rematch. Fewer than 3,000 fans were in attendance at the bout which was held in Lewiston, Maine.

Trivia Answer: Jesse Owens

MAY

26

Today's Trivia: On May 26, 1987, the Celtics took Game 5 of the Eastern Conference Finals from the Pistons. Down by one, *"There's a steal by Bird! Underneath to DJ, who lays it in!...Right at one second left!"* Who made the famous call?

Birthdays: Brent Musburger, 1939; Darrell Evans, 1947; Wesley Walker, 1955; Rob Murphy, 1960; Steve Pate, 1961; Greg Lloyd, 1965; Jason Bere, 1971; Travis Lee, 1975; Ben Zobrist, 1981

On This Day: In 1959, Pirates pitcher Harvey Haddix was perfect for 12 innings, but it wasn't good enough. A throwing error, an intentional walk and a double were enough to allow the Braves to get by the Pirates and Haddix, 1-0, in 13 innings.

Trivia Answer: Johnny Most

MAY

27

Today's Trivia: On May 27, 1968, who officially called it a career after four decades as the head coach of the Chicago Bears?

Birthdays: Sam Snead, 1912; Terry Collins, 1949; Jackie Slater, 1954; John Jaha, 1966; Jeff Bagwell, 1968; Frank Thomas, 1968; Todd Hundley, 1969; Antonio Freeman, 1972; Danny Wuerffel, 1974; Brad Boxberger, 1988

On This Day: In 1985, Kentucky Derby winner Spend A Buck made a buck and then some, winning the largest purse in horse racing history. Spend A Buck beat Creme Fraiche in a photo finish at the Jersey Derby to collect the winner's check of $2.6 million. The record stood for nearly 20 years, until Smarty Jones won the 2004 Kentucky Derby and a $5 million bonus.

Trivia Answer: George Halas

MAY

Today's Trivia: On May 28, 1956, what Pirate set a new MLB record by homering in his eighth consecutive game?

Birthdays: Jim Thorpe, 1888; Jerry West, 1938; Terry Crisp, 1943; Ron Wilson, 1955; Kirk Gibson, 1957; Ben Howland, 1957; Armon Gilliam, 1964; Glen Rice, 1967; Jhonny Peralta, 1982; Michael Oher, 1986; NaVorro Bowman, 1988; Craig Kimbrel, 1988

On This Day: In 1951, after going 0-for-12 to start his career, Willie Mays hit his first big league home run. Exactly 55 years later, Mays' godson, Barry Bonds, would pass Babe Ruth after hitting his 715th career homer.

Trivia Answer: Dale Long
(Don Mattingly and Ken Griffey Jr. would later match the mark.)

MAY

Today's Trivia: On May 29, 1984, the Boston Red Sox retired what uniform number of Ted Williams?

Birthdays: Tony Zale, 1913; Richie Guerin, 1932; Fay Vincent, 1938; Al Unser, 1939; Blue Moon Odom, 1945; Eric Davis, 1962; Jerry Hairston, Jr., 1976; Shaun King, 1977; Carmelo Anthony, 1984; Trevor Rosenthal, 1990; Steven Matz, 1991

On This Day: In 2001, the U.S. Supreme Court ruled that the Americans with Disabilities Act required the PGA Tour to allow Casey Martin to ride in a golf cart between shots. Martin was born with a defect in his right leg known as Klippel-Trenaunay-Weber syndrome, which causes severe swelling and pain.

Trivia Answer: 9

MAY 30

Today's Trivia: On May 30, 1993, Brazilian Emerson Fittipaldi won the Indianapolis 500 and proceeded to anger fans when he drank a glass of orange juice rather than what traditional beverage?

Birthdays: Gale Sayers, 1943; Lydell Mitchell, 1949; Billy Donovan, 1965; Manny Ramirez, 1972; Tony Watson, 1985; Zack Wheeler, 1990; Harrison Barnes, 1992

On This Day: In 1911, Ray Harroun won the first Indianapolis 500 with a blistering average speed of 74.6 miles per hour. It took Harroun nearly seven hours to complete the race.

Trivia Answer: Milk

MAY 31

Today's Trivia: On May 31, 1937, the Dodgers put an end to the historic 24-game winning streak of what Giants Hall of Fame pitcher?

Birthdays: Happy Hairston, 1942; Joe Namath, 1943; Jim Craig, 1957; Joe Orsulak, 1962; Kenny Lofton, 1967; Dave Roberts, 1972; Jake Peavy, 1981; Andrew Bailey, 1984; Nate Robinson, 1984; Jordy Nelson, 1985

On This Day: In 1983, Moses Malone led the Philadelphia 76ers to a 115-108 win over the Los Angeles Lakers and a four-game sweep of the championship series. Malone was the series' Most Valuable Player, as well as the regular season MVP for the second year in a row.

Trivia Answer: Carl Hubbell

JUNE

Today's Trivia: On June 1, 2012, who pitched the first no-hitter in the history of the New York Mets?

Birthdays: Alan Ameche, 1933; Dean Chance, 1941; Paul Coffey, 1961; Alexi Lalas, 1970; Derek Lowe, 1973; Santana Moss, 1979; Carlos Zambrano, 1981; Justine Henin, 1982; Nick Young, 1985

On This Day: In 1986, Pat Bradley won the LPGA Championship by sinking a birdie putt on the final hole. In doing so, she became the first golfer to win all four modern major women's tournaments.

Trivia Answer: Johan Santana

JUNE

Today's Trivia: On June 2, 2007, the LeBron James-led Cleveland Cavaliers reached the NBA Finals for the first time in franchise history by taking out the Pistons in six games. They would be swept, however, by what team in the title round?

Birthdays: Johnny Weissmuller, 1904; Tex Schramm, 1920; Larry Jackson, 1931; Garo Yepremian, 1944; Larry Robinson, 1951; Gary Bettman, 1952; Craig Stadler, 1953; Bryan Harvey, 1963; Mike Stanton, 1967; Raul Ibanez, 1972; Neifi Perez, 1973; Abby Wambach, 1980; Freddy Adu, 1989; Eddie Lacy, 1990

On This Day: In 1935, the playing career of Babe Ruth came to an end. The Boston Braves gave the 40-year-old slugger his unconditional release, 21 years after he broke in with the crosstown Red Sox as a pitcher. Exactly six years later, another legacy would come to a more tragic end as Lou Gehrig died at the age of 37.

Trivia Answer: San Antonio Spurs

JUNE

Today's Trivia: On June 3, 1888, *The San Francisco Examiner* published what now-legendary poem written by Ernest Lawrence Thayer?

Birthdays: Jim Gentile, 1934; Billy Cunningham, 1943; Emmitt Thomas, 1943; Hale Irwin, 1945; Frank Tanana, 1953; Ibrahim Hussein, 1958; Sam Mills, 1959; Steve Lyons, 1960; Carl Everett, 1971; Jose Molina, 1975; Jan-Michael Gambill, 1977; Travis Hafner, 1977; Al Horford, 1986; Rafael Nadal, 1986; Yordano Ventura, 1991

On This Day: In 1932, Lou Gehrig made history by hitting four consecutive home runs in a game. Exactly five years later, legend has it that Negro League star Josh Gibson clubbed a home run at Yankee Stadium that traveled approximately 580 feet.

Trivia Answer: Casey at the Bat

JUNE

Today's Trivia: On June 4, 1976, the Celtics outlasted what team, 128-126, in a triple overtime classic in Game 5 of the NBA Finals?

Birthdays: Bobby Wanzer, 1921; Art Mahaffey, 1938; Sandra Haynie, 1943; Terry Kennedy, 1956; Tony Pena, 1957; Xavier McDaniel, 1963; Darin Erstad, 1974; Greg Monroe, 1990

On This Day: In 1987, track and field's longest winning streak came to a stumbling end. Edwin Moses clipped the final hurdle in the 400 meters, allowing fellow American Danny Harris to cross the finish line just ahead of him. Moses had won 122 straight races over almost 10 years.

Trivia Answer: Phoenix Suns (Boston would win the series in six.)

JUNE

Today's Trivia: On June 5, 1993, who became the first female jockey to win a Triple Crown race?

Birthdays: Marion Motley, 1920; Art Donovan, 1925; Robert Kraft, 1941; John Carlos, 1945; Bob Probert, 1965; Ray Lankford, 1967; Russ Ortiz, 1974; Zydrunas Ilgauskas, 1975; Torry Holt, 1976; Marques Colston, 1983

On This Day: In 1977, the Portland Trail Blazers beat the Philadelphia 76ers, 109-107, to win their first NBA title. Portland did it the hard way, winning four straight games after losing the first two. Bill Walton earned MVP honors.

Trivia Answer: Julie Krone, when she rode Colonial Affair to victory at the Belmont Stakes

---

JUNE

Today's Trivia: On June 6, 1992, who broke Mickey Mantle's record for career RBIs by a switch-hitter?

Birthdays: Bill Dickey, 1907; Bobby Mitchell, 1935; Ed Giacomin, 1939; Bud Harrelson, 1944; Tommie Smith, 1944; Bjorn Borg, 1956; Cam Neely, 1965; Mark Ellis, 1977; Jeremy Affeldt, 1979; DeAndre Hopkins, 1992

On This Day: In 2015, American Pharoah claimed victory at the Belmont Stakes to become the first horse to win the Triple Crown since Affirmed in 1978. Victor Espinoza, at age 43, became the oldest jockey to win the Triple Crown.

Trivia Answer: Eddie Murray

JUNE

Today's Trivia: On June 7, 1998, what team did the Chicago Bulls destroy, 96-54, for the most lopsided win in NBA Finals history?

Birthdays: James J. Braddock, 1905; Rocky Graziano, 1922; Herb Score, 1933; Cazzie Russell, 1944; Don Money, 1947; Thurman Munson, 1947; Heathcliff Slocumb, 1966; Terance Mathis, 1967; Mike Modano, 1970; Allen Iverson, 1975; Anna Kournikova, 1981

On This Day: In 1941, Whirlaway won the Belmont Stakes by two and a half lengths. This victory marked the first of two Triple Crowns collected by jockey Eddie Arcaro in his career.

Trivia Answer: Utah Jazz

JUNE

Today's Trivia: On June 8, 1961, what MLB team set a new record with four consecutive home runs in a game, courtesy of Eddie Mathews, Hank Aaron, Joe Adcock and Frank Thomas?

Birthdays: Byron "Whizzer" White, 1917; Del Ennis, 1925; Herb Adderley, 1939; Mark Belanger, 1944; Butch Reynolds, 1964; Troy Vincent, 1971; Lindsay Davenport, 1976; Kenji Johjima, 1976; Kim Clijsters, 1983

On This Day: In 1966, the battle between the AFL and NFL came to an end with the announcement of the merger of the leagues. While the first "Super Bowl" would take place at the end of the season, it would not be until 1970 that the two leagues became one.

Trivia Answer: Milwaukee Braves

JUNE

Today's Trivia: On June 9, 1973, what Triple Crown winner won the Belmont Stakes by an astounding 31 lengths?

Birthdays: Bill Virdon, 1931; Dick Vitale, 1939; Dave Parker, 1951; Billy Knight, 1952; Wayman Tisdale, 1964; Tedy Bruschi, 1973; Randy Winn, 1974; Olin Kreutz, 1977; Peja Stojakovic, 1977; Heather Mitts, 1978

On This Day: In 1993, the Montreal Canadiens defeated Wayne Gretzky and the L.A. Kings in five games to win the Stanley Cup. Montreal claimed its 24th title on the 100th anniversary of the first awarding of the Cup. They remain the last Canadian team to win it all.

Trivia Answer: Secretariat

JUNE

Today's Trivia: On June 10, 1944, what 15-year-old became the youngest player in Major League history when he debuted as a pitcher for the Cincinnati Reds?

Birthdays: Ken Singleton, 1947; Dan Fouts, 1951; Brent Sutter, 1962; Pokey Reese, 1973; Tara Lipinski, 1982; Marion Barber, 1983; Jose Reyes, 1983; Kyle Williams, 1983; Jeff Teague, 1988

On This Day: In 2000, the New Jersey Devils won their second Stanley Cup by defeating the Dallas Stars in six games. The thrilling series featured four one-goal games, including the double-overtime clincher in which Jason Arnott scored the Cup-winner.

Trivia Answer: Joe Nuxhall

JUNE

Today's Trivia: On June 11, 2012, what team won the Stanley Cup after a postseason run in which they suffered just two losses in 14 games before the Finals?

Birthdays: Ernie Nevers, 1903; Vince Lombardi, 1913; Frank Thomas, 1929; Jackie Stewart, 1939; Dave Cash, 1948; Joe Montana, 1956; Brock Marion, 1970; Odalis Perez, 1978; Diana Taurasi, 1982; Jose Reyes, 1983; Brock Holt, 1988; Maya Moore, 1989

On This Day: In 1950, Ben Hogan defeated Lloyd Mangrum and George Fazio in an 18-hole playoff to win his second U.S. Open. The previous year, Hogan survived a near-fatal car crash and doctors feared he'd never walk again, let alone play golf.

Trivia Answer: Los Angeles Kings, who beat the New Jersey Devils in six games

---

JUNE

Today's Trivia: On June 12, 2009, Pittsburgh won Game 7 over the Red Wings and claimed the Stanley Cup. What Penguin became the first Russian-born player to win the Conn Smythe Trophy as the MVP of the playoffs?

Birthdays: Marv Albert, 1941; Mario Soto, 1956; Ryan Klesko, 1971; Kerry Kittles, 1974; Hideki Matsui, 1974; Antawn Jamison, 1976; Dallas Clark, 1979; Jrue Holiday, 1990; Avisail Garcia, 1991

On This Day: In 1991, the Chicago Bulls won their first NBA championship after they beat the Los Angeles Lakers, 108-101, to take the series in five games. In addition to getting his first of six rings, Michael Jordan was named Finals MVP for the first of six times.

Trivia Answer: Evgeni Malkin

JUNE 13

Today's Trivia: On June 13, 1994, what Chicago Cub announced his sudden retirement from the game, forfeiting approximately $16 million that remained on his contract?

Birthdays: Paavo Nurmi, 1897; Red Grange, 1903; Don Budge, 1915; Mel Parnell, 1922; Ernie Whitt, 1952; Hannah Storm, 1962; Sarunas Marciulionis, 1964; Sam Adams, 1973; Valeri Bure, 1974; Jonathan Lucroy, 1986; Ryan McDonagh, 1989; Hassan Whiteside, 1989

On This Day: In 1935, in one of the greatest upsets in boxing history, James J. Braddock won a unanimous decision over Max Baer to become the heavyweight champion. His story would be the inspiration behind the 2005 movie *Cinderella Man*.

Trivia Answer: Ryne Sandberg

JUNE 14

Today's Trivia: On June 14, 1990, it was The Microwave to the rescue. Who knocked down a jumper with .7 seconds left to give the Pistons a Game 5 win, and the NBA championship, over the Blazers?

Birthdays: Don Newcombe, 1926; Pat Summitt, 1952; Eric Heiden, 1958; Sam Perkins, 1961; Steffi Graf, 1969; Bruce Bowen, 1971; Chris McAlister, 1977; Sammy Watkins, 1993; Jaylon Smith, 1995

On This Day: In 1994, the curse was broken as the New York Rangers won the Stanley Cup for the first time since 1940. New York beat Vancouver, 3-2, in Game 7 of the Finals after squandering a three-games-to-one lead.

Trivia Answer: Vinnie Johnson

JUNE

15

Today's Trivia: On June 15, 1977, the New York Mets received little in return when they dealt what future Hall of Famer in the prime of his career to the Reds?

Birthdays: Billy Williams, 1938; Mike Holmgren, 1948; Dusty Baker, 1949; Lance Parrish, 1956; Brett Butler, 1957; Wade Boggs, 1958; Tony Clark, 1972; Justin Leonard, 1972; Andy Pettitte, 1972; Tim Lincecum, 1984; Cliff Pennington, 1984; Mike Fiers, 1985

On This Day: In 1938, Cincinnati's Johnny Vander Meer threw his second straight no-hitter, shutting out the Dodgers, 6-0. Four days earlier, Vander Meer had no-hit Boston, 3-0. The feat of consecutive "no-nos" has yet to be matched.

Trivia Answer: Tom Seaver

JUNE

16

Today's Trivia: On June 16, 2015, the Golden State Warriors won their first title in 40 years with a Game 6 triumph over the Cleveland Cavs. What player, who began the Finals coming off the bench, was the MVP of the series?

Birthdays: Rick Adelman, 1946; Al Cowlings, 1947; Roberto Duran, 1951; Darrell Griffith, 1958; Wally Joyner, 1962; Phil Mickelson, 1970; Chris Gomez, 1976; Kerry Wood, 1977; Joe Saunders, 1981; Jonathan Broxton, 1984; Jermaine Gresham, 1988

On This Day: In 2008, a hobbled Tiger Woods won his third U.S. Open by beating Rocco Mediate on the first hole of a sudden-death playoff following an 18-hole playoff. Woods would go on to call the triumph "my greatest ever championship."

Trivia Answer: Andre Iguodala

JUNE

Today's Trivia: On June 17, 1994, what sporting event was forced into a small split-screen box on NBC as coverage of the infamous O.J. Simpson Bronco chase took over?

Birthdays: Elroy "Crazylegs" Hirsch, 1923; Maurice Stokes, 1933; Bobby Bell, 1940; Dave Concepcion, 1948; Mike Milbury, 1952; Dermontti Dawson, 1965; Dan Jansen, 1965; Jason Hanson, 1970; Venus Williams, 1980; Albert Haynesworth, 1981; Amari Cooper, 1994

On This Day: In 2008, the Boston Celtics were once again NBA champs after a 22-year drought. They destroyed the Lakers, 131-92, to win it in six. Exactly two years later, L.A. would win a Finals rematch with a come-from-behind Game 7 victory, 83-79.

Trivia Answer: Game 5 of the NBA Finals between the Knicks and Rockets

---

JUNE

Today's Trivia: On June 18, 2000, who won the 100th U.S. Open by a staggering 15 strokes?

Birthdays: George Mikan, 1924; Lou Brock, 1939; Romeo Crennel, 1947; Andres Galarraga, 1961; Bruce Smith, 1963; Sandy Alomar, Jr., 1966; Jeff Saturday, 1975; Martin St. Louis, 1975; Antonio Gates, 1980; Jason Castro, 1987; Matt Moore, 1989

On This Day: In 1960, Arnold Palmer rallied from a seven-stroke deficit at the start of the final round to win his only U.S. Open. Palmer finished two strokes ahead of 20-year-old amateur Jack Nicklaus.

Trivia Answer: Tiger Woods

JUNE

19

Today's Trivia: On June 19, 1999, the Dallas Stars won their first Stanley Cup by defeating the Buffalo Sabres, 2-1, in triple overtime of Game 6. Who scored the controversial game-winner?

Birthdays: Lou Gehrig, 1903; Leo Nomellini, 1924; Shirley Muldowney, 1940; Jerry Reuss, 1949; Doug Mientkiewicz, 1974; Patrick Surtain, 1976; Bruce Chen, 1977; Peter Warrick, 1977; Dirk Nowitzki, 1978; Marvin Williams, 1986; Jacob deGrom, 1988; Devin Mesoraco, 1988; Oscar Taveras, 1992

On This Day: In 2016, the Cavaliers defeated the Warriors, 93-89, in Game 7 of the NBA Finals. A triple-double in the clincher by Series MVP LeBron James brought an end to a 52-year major sports championship drought in Cleveland.

Trivia Answer: Brett Hull (Replays showed his skate was in the crease, while the puck was not.)

JUNE

20

Today's Trivia: On June 20, 1993, the Bulls claimed a "three-peat" after what player hit a title-winning three-pointer in the final seconds of Game 6 against the Suns?

Birthdays: Doris Hart, 1925; Len Dawson, 1935; Andy Etchebarren, 1943; Dickie Thon, 1958; Carlos Lee, 1976; LaVar Arrington, 1978; Kendrys Morales, 1983; Darren Sproles, 1983; Darko Milicic, 1985

On This Day: In 1960, Floyd Patterson knocked out Ingemar Johansson in the fifth round to regain his heavyweight title, the first boxer in history to do so. Johansson had KO'd Patterson a year earlier to take the crown.

Trivia Answer: John Paxson

JUNE

21

Today's Trivia: On June 21, 1997, the New York Liberty defeated the Los Angeles Sparks in the first game in the history of what league?

Birthdays: Eddie Lopat, 1918; Wade Phillips, 1947; Rick Sutcliffe, 1956; Tom Chambers, 1959; Mike Bordick, 1965; Derrick Coleman, 1967; Al Wilson, 1977; Richard Jefferson, 1980; Thaddeus Young, 1988

On This Day: In 1964, Jim Bunning, a father of seven at the time, celebrated Father's Day by throwing a perfect game against the Mets. The Phillies right-hander shut down New York, 6-0, for the National League's first perfect game in 84 years.

Trivia Answer: WNBA

JUNE

22

Today's Trivia: On June 22, 1986, whose "Hand of God" goal helped Argentina defeat England in the World Cup quarterfinals?

Birthdays: Carl Hubbell, 1903; Davey O'Brien, 1917; Pete Maravich, 1947; Clyde Drexler, 1962; Kurt Warner, 1971; Champ Bailey, 1978; Brad Hawpe, 1979; Ian Kinsler, 1982; Jason Motte, 1982; Dustin Johnson, 1984; Danny Green, 1987

On This Day: In 1937, Joe Louis began boxing's longest reign as heavyweight champ. He took the crown from James J. Braddock and kept it for over 11 years. One year later to the day, Louis avenged his only loss to date by knocking out Max Schmeling in the first round.

Trivia Answer: Diego Maradona

JUNE

23

Today's Trivia: On June 23, 1972, what revolutionary piece of legislation that opened doors for women in sports was signed into law by President Richard Nixon?

Birthdays: Wilma Rudolph, 1940; Filbert Bayi, 1953; Robert Brooks, 1970; Felix Potvin, 1971; Zinedine Zidane, 1972; Mark Hendrickson, 1974; LaDainian Tomlinson, 1979

On This Day: In 2005, the San Antonio Spurs stopped the Detroit Pistons from winning consecutive titles with an 81-74 Game 7 victory. It was the third title for San Antonio, as well as the third time Tim Duncan was named NBA Finals MVP.

Trivia Answer: Title IX

JUNE

24

Today's Trivia: On June 24, 2013, a rare Stanley Cup Finals between two Original Six teams came to an end as what squad defeated the Bruins to win the title in six?

Birthdays: Jack Dempsey, 1895; Billy Casper, 1931; Sam Jones, 1933; Don Mincher, 1938; Wayne Cashman, 1945; Doug Jones, 1957; John Tortorella, 1958; Juli Inkster, 1960; Antoine Winfield, 1977; J.J. Redick, 1984; Phil Hughes, 1986; Lionel Messi, 1987; Mo'ne Davis, 2001

On This Day: In 2010, John Isner beat Nicolas Mahut at Wimbledon in the longest match in tennis history. The 11 hours and five minutes of play spanned three days, with the match finishing 6-4, 3-6, 6-7 (7), 7-6 (3), 70-68 (183 games).

Trivia Answer: Chicago Blackhawks

JUNE

Today's Trivia: On June 25, 1968, what Giants rookie became the first 20th century player to hit a grand slam in his big league debut?

Birthdays: Sandy Saddler, 1926; Willis Reed, 1942; Phyllis George, 1949; Mike Stanley, 1963; Dell Curry, 1964; Dikembe Mutombo, 1966; Aaron Sele, 1970; Billy Wagner, 1971; Carlos Delgado, 1972; Aramis Ramirez, 1978; Matt Schaub, 1981; Paul Maholm, 1982

On This Day: In 1978, Argentina upended the Netherlands, 3-1, to win its first World Cup. The host team celebrated before a sellout crowd in Buenos Aires as well as a worldwide television audience estimated at one billion people.

Trivia Answer: Bobby Bonds

JUNE

Today's Trivia: On June 26, 2002, for the first time ever, someone who played neither high school nor college basketball in the United States was made the #1 pick of the NBA Draft. Who?

Birthdays: Abner Doubleday, 1819; Babe Didrikson Zaharias, 1911; Hal Greer, 1936; Greg LeMond, 1961; Jerome Kersey, 1962; Shannon Sharpe, 1968; Derek Jeter, 1974; Jason Kendall, 1974; Chad Pennington, 1976; Michael Vick, 1980; Raymond Felton, 1984; Deron Williams, 1984; Rudy Gobert, 1992

On This Day: In 1916, the Cleveland Indians became the first baseball players with numbers on their uniforms. The Tribe wore the numerals on their sleeves. Meanwhile, on the same day in New York, three fans were arrested for petty larceny at the Polo Grounds when they refused to return baseballs hit into the stands.

Trivia Answer: Yao Ming

JUNE

Today's Trivia: On June 27, 2003, what team hammered the Marlins, 25-8, and scored 10 runs before recording their first offensive out of the game?

Birthdays: Willie Mosconi, 1913; Gus Zernial, 1923; Rico Petrocelli, 1943; Craig Hodges, 1960; Chuck Person, 1964; Jeff Conine, 1966; Jim Edmonds, 1970; Julius Thomas, 1988; Bobby Wagner, 1990

On This Day: In 1988, Mike Tyson made short work of Michael Spinks to retain his heavyweight title. How short? The champ knocked out Spinks in 91 seconds.

Trivia Answer: Boston Red Sox

JUNE

Today's Trivia: On June 28, 2007, two future Hall of Famers reached career milestones – one with his 500th home run and the other his 3,000th hit. Who are they?

Birthdays: Chuck Howley, 1936; Al Downing, 1941; Don Baylor, 1949; John Elway, 1960; Jeff Malone, 1961; Mark Grace, 1964; Bobby Hurley, 1971; Marvin Jones, 1972; Corey Koskie, 1973; Brandon Phillips, 1981; Bradley Beal, 1993

On This Day: In 1997, Mike Tyson bit off more than he could chew when he was disqualified from his heavyweight championship bout vs. Evander Holyfield. In the third round, a frustrated Tyson chomped down on both of Holyfield's ears. The fight would be called, and Tyson would temporarily lose his boxing license.

Trivia Answer: Frank Thomas and Craig Biggio, respectively

JUNE 29

Today's Trivia: On June 29, 1990, a baseball anomaly occurred when pitchers from both leagues threw no-hitters. What A's and Dodgers hurlers made history?

Birthdays: Harmon Killebrew, 1936; Dan Dierdorf, 1949; Rick Honeycutt, 1954; Pedro Guerrero, 1956; Joe Johnson, 1981; Kawhi Leonard, 1991

On This Day: In 1958, a 17-year-old phenom named Pele scored twice as he led Brazil over Sweden, 5-2, to win the country's first World Cup. In all, Pele scored six goals in the tournament.

Trivia Answer: Dave Stewart and Fernando Valenzuela, respectively

---

JUNE 30

Today's Trivia: On June 30, 1993, the Orlando Magic selected Chris Webber #1 overall in the NBA Draft before dealing him to Golden State in exchange for what fellow draftee?

Birthdays: Ron Swoboda, 1944; Tubby Smith, 1951; Roy Green, 1957; Tony Fernandez, 1962; Mitch Richmond, 1965; Mike Tyson, 1966; Mark Grudzielanek, 1970; Garret Anderson, 1972; Chan Ho Park, 1973; Miles Austin, 1984; Michael Phelps, 1985

On This Day: In 1984, the Los Angeles Express and Michigan Panthers of the USFL played a postseason contest that turned into the longest game in pro football history. The teams went into a third overtime before the Express won, 27-21, after 93 minutes and 33 seconds of playing time.

Trivia Answer: Anfernee Hardaway

JULY

Today's Trivia: On July 1, 1910, what Chicago sports venue, that remained open until 1990, held its first game?

Birthdays: Bob Prince, 1916; Rod Gilbert, 1941; Mike Haynes, 1953; Nancy Lieberman, 1958; Carl Lewis, 1961; Eric Ball, 1966; Jarome Iginla, 1977; Nelson Cruz, 1980; Chris Perez, 1985; Michael Wacha, 1991

On This Day: In 1951, Bob Feller became the first modern-era pitcher to hurl three no-hitters, with a 2-1 win over the Tigers. Exactly 39 years later, Yankees pitcher Andy Hawkins no-hit the White Sox, but because of a series of errors, wound up losing the game, 4-0.

Trivia Answer: Comiskey Park (originally White Sox Park)

JULY

Today's Trivia: On July 2, 1921, over 80,000 watched in New Jersey as what "Manassa Mauler" knocked out Georges Carpentier in boxing's first-ever $1,000,000 gate?

Birthdays: René Lacoste, 1904; Richard Petty, 1937; Tony Armas, 1953; Clark Kellogg, 1961; Jose Canseco, 1964; So Taguchi, 1969; Troy Brown, 1971; Sean Casey, 1974; Joe Thornton, 1979; Nyjer Morgan, 1980; Angel Pagan, 1981; Wladimir Balentien, 1984; Johnny Weir, 1984; Brett Cecil, 1986; Alex Morgan, 1989

On This Day: In 1938, Helen Wills Moody defeated Helen Hull Jacobs to win the Wimbledon Championship for the eighth time. Fifty years later to the day, Steffi Graf beat Martina Navratilova for her first Wimbledon title. Navratilova, meanwhile, would top Moody's mark with her ninth Wimbledon win in 1990.

Trivia Answer: Jack Dempsey

JULY

Today's Trivia: On July 3, 1966, what Braves hurler became the only pitcher ever to hit two grand slams in a single game?

Birthdays: Buddy Rosar, 1914; Mike Burton, 1947; Elmo Wright, 1949; Frank Tanana, 1953; Greg Vaughn, 1965; Moises Alou, 1966; Neil O'Donnell, 1966; Brian Cashman, 1967; Teemu Selanne, 1970; Edinson Volquez, 1983; Jordan Reed, 1990

On This Day: In 1983, sprinter Calvin Smith broke the record for the men's 100-meter dash. The same day, at the same Colorado Springs track meet and in a span of just 15 minutes, Evelyn Ashford snapped the women's 100-meter mark.

Trivia Answer: Tony Cloninger

JULY

Today's Trivia: On July 4, 1981, who claimed his first Wimbledon title by ending the five-year reign of Bjorn Borg?

Birthdays: Abe Saperstein, 1902; Al Davis, 1929; George Steinbrenner, 1930; Digger Phelps, 1941; Floyd Little, 1942; Emerson Boozer, 1943; Bobby Cremins, 1947; Pam Shriver, 1962; Harvey & Horace Grant, 1965; Vinny Castilla, 1967; Brendan Donnelly, 1971; La'Roi Glover, 1974

On This Day: In 1939, Yankee fans packed the Stadium to pay tribute to Lou Gehrig. The ailing "Iron Horse" bid farewell to his teammates and fans with an emotional speech in which he called himself "the luckiest man on the face of the earth."

Trivia Answer: John McEnroe

JULY

Today's Trivia: On July 5, 2009, who broke Pete Sampras' record when he won his 15th Grand Slam title by defeating Andy Roddick at Wimbledon in five sets?

Birthdays: John McKay, 1923; Gary Matthews, 1950; Goose Gossage, 1951; Johnny Rodgers, 1951; James Lofton, 1956; Doug Wilson, 1957; John LeClair, 1969; Amélie Mauresmo, 1979; Jesse Crain, 1981

On This Day: In 1975, Arthur Ashe became the first African-American to win the men's singles title at Wimbledon when he defeated Jimmy Connors in four sets. Twenty-eight years earlier to the day, Larry Doby broke the color barrier in the American League, appearing as a pinch-hitter for the Cleveland Indians.

Trivia Answer: Roger Federer

JULY

Today's Trivia: On July 6, 1983, what Angel hit the first and only grand slam in All-Star Game history?

Birthdays: Fred Dryer, 1946; Brad Park, 1948; Willie Randolph, 1954; Joe Jacoby, 1959; Valerie Brisco, 1960; Lance Johnson, 1963; Alvin Harper, 1968; Pau Gasol, 1980; Nnamdi Asomugha, 1981; Manny Machado, 1992

On This Day: In 1933, players from the National League and the American League squared off for baseball's first All-Star Game at Comiskey Park. Babe Ruth's two-run homer led the AL to a 4-2 victory.

Trivia Answer: Fred Lynn

JULY

Today's Trivia: On July 7, 1978, the NBA approved a rare swap when Irv Levin gave up what legendary franchise to John Y. Brown in order to acquire the Buffalo Braves?

Birthdays: Satchel Paige, 1906; Dan Gladden, 1957; Ralph Sampson, 1960; Chuck Knoblauch, 1968; Joe Sakic, 1969; Lisa Leslie, 1972; Michael Westbrook, 1972; Jose Jimenez, 1973; Chris Andersen, 1978; Michelle Kwan, 1980; Brandon McCarthy, 1983

On This Day: In 1985, 17-year-old Boris Becker became the youngest player and the first unseeded player to win at Wimbledon, beating Kevin Curren in four sets. Exactly 28 years later, Andy Murray became the first Brit to win at Wimbledon in nearly 80 years when he defeated Novak Djokovic in the final.

Trivia Answer: Boston Celtics

JULY

Today's Trivia: On July 8, 2014, what country embarrassed host Brazil, 7-1, in the World Cup semifinals, before going on to defeat Argentina to win it all?

Birthdays: Harrison Dillard, 1923; Roone Arledge, 1931; John David Crow, 1935; Jack Lambert, 1952; Jerome Walton, 1965; Eric Chouinard, 1980; Hakim Warrick, 1982; Jaime Garcia, 1986; Josh Harrison, 1987

On This Day: In 1889, John L. Sullivan knocked out Jake Kilrain in the 75th round to win the heavyweight championship. The fight, considered to be a turning point in boxing history, was the last of the bare-knuckle bouts.

Trivia Answer: Germany

JULY

Today's Trivia: On July 9, 2002, the MLB All-Star Game ended in a 7-7 tie after 11 innings. Why did commissioner Bud Selig call off the game?

Birthdays: Jim Pollard, 1922; Red Kelly, 1927; O.J. Simpson, 1947; Willie Wilson, 1955; Jim Paxson, 1957; Trent Green, 1970; Miguel Montero, 1983

On This Day: In 1966, Jack Nicklaus won his first British Open, shooting a 282. The one-stroke victory was a historic one, as it completed the first of his three career grand slams.

Trivia Answer: Both teams ran out of available pitchers.

JULY

Today's Trivia: On July 10, 1999, the U.S. women won the World Cup over China in thrilling fashion. After a scoreless regulation and overtime, whose dramatic shootout goal gave her team a 5-4 win on penalty kicks?

Birthdays: Jake LaMotta, 1921; Arthur Ashe, 1943; Hal McRae, 1945; Virginia Wade, 1945; Chico Resch, 1948; Andre Dawson, 1954; Roger Craig, 1960; Urban Meyer, 1964; Antonio Brown, 1988; Trent Richardson, 1990

On This Day: In 1934, future Hall of Famer Carl Hubbell put on quite a show at the second annual All-Star Game. The Giants pitcher fanned Babe Ruth, Lou Gehrig, Jimmie Foxx, Al Simmons and Joe Cronin consecutively over two innings. However, the American League still prevailed, 9-7.

Trivia Answer: Brandi Chastain

JULY

Today's Trivia: On July 11, 1989, what former U.S. President shared the NBC broadcast booth with Vin Scully during the MLB All-Star Game?

Birthdays: Bob Allison, 1934; Lou Hudson, 1944; Leon Spinks, 1953; Brent Sutter, 1962; Al MacInnis, 1963; Rod Strickland, 1966; Andy Ashby, 1967; Javier Lopez, 1977; Andre Johnson, 1981; Chris Cooley, 1982; Joe Pavelski, 1984; Patrick Peterson, 1990; Caroline Wozniacki, 1990; Joey Bosa, 1995

On This Day: In 1914, George Herman "Babe" Ruth made his Major League debut. The 19-year-old pitched seven innings as his Boston Red Sox defeated Cleveland, 4-3.

Trivia Answer: Ronald Reagan

JULY

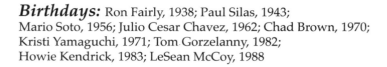

Today's Trivia: On July 12, 1998, what host country, behind two goals from Zinedine Zidane, upset Brazil, 3-0, to win their first-ever World Cup?

Birthdays: Ron Fairly, 1938; Paul Silas, 1943; Mario Soto, 1956; Julio Cesar Chavez, 1962; Chad Brown, 1970; Kristi Yamaguchi, 1971; Tom Gorzelanny, 1982; Howie Kendrick, 1983; LeSean McCoy, 1988

On This Day: In 1964, Mickey Wright won a playoff over Ruth Jessen to capture her fourth and final U.S. Women's Open golf tournament. Wright and Betsy Rawls remain the only four-time winners of the Open.

Trivia Answer: France

JULY

13

Today's Trivia: On July 13, 1963, what 43-year-old Indians pitcher won the 300th and final game of his MLB career?

Birthdays: Jack Kemp, 1935; Bob McKillop, 1950; David Thompson, 1954; Michael Spinks, 1956; Spud Webb, 1963; Yadier Molina, 1982; Shin-Soo Choo, 1982; DJ LeMahieu, 1988; Dante Exum, 1995

On This Day: In 1930, the first World Cup got underway. The first two matches took place simultaneously, with France and the U.S. coming out on top. In all, 13 teams entered the tournament, which would be won by the host nation, Uruguay.

Trivia Answer: Early Wynn

JULY

14

Today's Trivia: On July 14, 1985, the Baltimore Stars defeated the Oakland Invaders at Giants Stadium in New Jersey to win the final title of what league that would fold the following year?

Birthdays: Bob Purkey, 1929; Rosey Grier, 1932; Lee Elder, 1934; Robin Ventura, 1967; Tim Hudson, 1975; Darrelle Revis, 1985; Conor McGregor, 1988; Shabazz Napier, 1991

On This Day: In 1951, Citation, the 1948 Triple Crown winner, captured the Hollywood Gold Cup in his final race, becoming the first thoroughbred to top a million dollars in career winnings. That same day at Monmouth Park in New Jersey, CBS televised the Molly Pitcher Handicap in color, a sports first.

Trivia Answer: USFL

JULY

15

Today's Trivia: On July 15, 2007, who became the first pro sports team in American history to lose 10,000 games?

Birthdays: Donn Clendenon, 1935; Alex Karras, 1935; John Stallworth, 1952; Barry Melrose, 1956; Sammy Winder, 1959; Barry Trotz, 1962; Carnell Lake, 1967; James Baldwin, 1971; Miguel Olivo, 1978; Jonathan Cheechoo, 1980; Damian Lillard, 1990; Derrick Favors, 1991; Tobias Harris, 1992

On This Day: In 1923, Bobby Jones edged Bobby Cruickshank by two strokes in an 18-hole playoff to win the U.S. Open. It was the first major title for the 21-year-old amateur and future golf legend.

Trivia Answer: Philadelphia Phillies

JULY

16

Today's Trivia: On July 16, 1948, what Dodgers manager stunned the baseball world when he announced he'd be leaving to join the rival New York Giants?

Birthdays: Shoeless Joe Jackson, 1887; Margaret Court, 1942; Jimmy Johnson, 1943; Gary Anderson, 1959; Terry Pendleton, 1960; Claude Lemieux, 1965; Charles Smith, 1965; Barry Sanders, 1968; Zach Randolph, 1981; Carli Lloyd, 1982; Duncan Keith, 1983

On This Day: In 1941, the Yankee Clipper, Joe DiMaggio, went 3-for-4 to extend his record consecutive game hitting streak to 56 games as New York defeated the Indians, 10-3. DiMaggio's historic streak would end the following night against Cleveland.

Trivia Answer: Leo Durocher

JULY

17

Today's Trivia: On July 17, 1994, Brazil won the first World Cup ever decided by penalty kicks. What Italian infamously missed the game-tying try that ended the contest?

Birthdays: Lou Boudreau, 1917; Juan Antonio Samaranch, 1920; Johnny "Red" Kerr, 1932; Bobby "Slick" Leonard, 1932; Daryle Lamonica, 1941; Connie Hawkins, 1942; Don Kessinger, 1942; Bryan Trottier, 1956; Bobby Thigpen, 1963; Eric Moulds, 1973; Jason Jennings, 1978; Ryan Miller, 1980; Steve Delabar, 1983; Adam Lind, 1983

On This Day: In 2005, Tiger Woods won his second Open Championship in decisive fashion. In claiming his tenth major, Woods became only the second golfer, after Jack Nicklaus, to win each major more than once.

Trivia Answer: Roberto Baggio

JULY

18

Today's Trivia: On July 18, 1999, David Cone pitched the 16th perfect game in MLB history. Ironically, it occurred the same day that the Yankees honored the man who caught Don Larsen's World Series perfecto in 1956. Who?

Birthdays: Dick Button, 1929; Joe Torre, 1940; Donald Fehr, 1948; Nick Faldo, 1957; Mike Greenwell, 1963; Dan O'Brien, 1966; Anfernee Hardaway, 1971; Torii Hunter, 1975; Ben Sheets, 1978; Deion Branch, 1979; Allen Craig, 1984; Jamie Benn, 1989

On This Day: In 1976, 14-year-old Nadia Comaneci of Romania recorded the first perfect score in Olympic gymnastics, a "10". When it was all over, Comaneci had tumbled her way to three gold medals for the uneven bars, balance beam and individual all-around.

Trivia Answer: Yogi Berra

JULY

19

Today's Trivia: On July 19, 1960, the "Dominican Daddy" made his MLB debut, shutting out the Phillies, 2-0, on just one hit. Who is the Hall of Fame pitcher?

Birthdays: Bob Meusel, 1896; Alex Hannum, 1923; Ilie Nastase, 1946; Billy Olson, 1958; Teresa Edwards, 1964; Stuart Scott, 1965; David Segui, 1966; LeRoy Butler, 1968; Vitali Klitschko, 1971; Preston Wilson, 1974; Rick Ankiel, 1979; Brent Grimes, 1983; Adam Morrison, 1984; LaMarcus Aldridge, 1985; Yan Gomes, 1987; Patrick Corbin, 1989

On This Day: In 1877, about 200 people were on hand to watch the first Wimbledon tennis championship. Britain's Spencer Gore prevailed out of the field of 21 competitors, taking home a 25-guinea trophy.

Trivia Answer: Juan Marichal

JULY

20

Today's Trivia: On July 20, 2015, Zach Johnson won the Open Championship in a playoff. The 2014 winner withdrew before the tournament due to injury, making it the first time in over 60 years that a defending champ was absent from the Open. Who was it?

Birthdays: Heinie Manush, 1901; Chuck Daly, 1930; Tony Oliva, 1938; Mel Daniels, 1944; Jake Scott, 1945; Mike Witt, 1960; Charles Johnson, 1971; Bengie Molina, 1974; Ray Allen, 1975; Pavel Datsyuk, 1978; Stephen Strasburg, 1988; Ben Simmons, 1996

On This Day: In 1969, Neil Armstrong and Buzz Aldrin landed on the moon. That same evening, pitcher Gaylord Perry hit his first Major League home run. Legend has it that several years prior, Perry's manager, Alvin Dark, joked that, "They'll put a man on the moon before he hits a home run." Perry would finish his career with six round-trippers.

Trivia Answer: Rory McIlroy

JULY

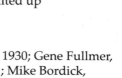

Today's Trivia: On July 21, 2007, David Beckham made his United States soccer debut when he suited up for what MLS squad?

Birthdays: Johnny Evers, 1881; Gene Littler, 1930; Gene Fullmer, 1931; Dave Henderson, 1958; Henry Ellard, 1961; Mike Bordick, 1965; Brandi Chastain, 1968; Geoff Jenkins, 1974; David Carr, 1979; Tamika Catchings, 1979; C.C. Sabathia, 1980; Wei-Yin Chen, 1985; DeAndre Jordan, 1988

On This Day: In 1979, Seve Ballesteros won his first British Open and the first of five majors, shooting a 283 at Royal Lytham, England. The Spaniard was three strokes better than Ben Crenshaw and Jack Nicklaus. Exactly 34 years later, Phil Mickelson would claim his first Open Championship and fifth major title.

Trivia Answer: LA Galaxy

JULY

Today's Trivia: On July 22, 2013, what former NL MVP did Major League Baseball suspend for the remainder of the season for violating the league's drug policy?

Birthdays: Ron Turcotte, 1941; Sparky Lyle, 1944; Lasse Viren, 1949; Dave Stieb, 1957; Alvin Robertson, 1962; Tim Brown, 1966; Keyshawn Johnson, 1972; Mike Sweeney, 1973; Scot Shields, 1975; Ryan Vogelsong, 1977; Steven Jackson, 1983; Ezekiel Elliott, 1995

On This Day: In 1990, Greg LeMond won cycling's Tour de France for the third time and second consecutive year. He finished 2 minutes and 16 seconds ahead of Claudio Chiappucci of Italy. In 1989, LeMond won by just eight seconds, the smallest margin of victory in the race's history. LeMond and Lance Armstrong remain the only Americans to claim victory in the race.

Trivia Answer: Ryan Braun

JULY

23

Today's Trivia: On July 23, 2000, Tiger Woods won the Open Championship to complete his first Grand Slam. Woods' -19 score was a record for all majors until who topped him with a -20 at the 2015 PGA Championship?

Birthdays: Pee Wee Reese, 1918; Don Drysdale, 1936; Ken Green, 1958; Gary Payton, 1968; Nomar Garciaparra, 1973; Terry Glenn, 1974; Maurice Greene, 1974; Matt Birk, 1976; Gerald Wallace, 1982; Brandon Roy, 1984

On This Day: In 1996, the U.S. women's gymnastics team won its first-ever team gold at the Summer Olympics in Atlanta. The "Magnificent Seven" received an inspirational performance from 4'8" Kerri Strug, who successfully landed her final vault despite hurting her ankle on the previous one. Her 9.712 score was good enough to clinch the gold.

Trivia Answer: Jason Day

JULY

24

Today's Trivia: On July 24, 2005, Lance Armstrong won his final Tour de France. While they have since been erased from the books, Armstrong finished his career with how many wins (all consecutively) in cycling's biggest race?

Birthdays: Willie Davis, 1934; Walt Bellamy, 1939; Steve Grogan, 1953; Joe Barry Carroll, 1958; Julie Krone, 1963; Karl Malone, 1963; Barry Bonds, 1964; Patrice Bergeron, 1985; Donte Whitner, 1985; Maurkice & Mike Pouncey, 1989

On This Day: In 1983, George Brett's two-out home run in the ninth gave the Royals a 5-4 lead over the Yankees. Swayed by New York manager Billy Martin, however, the umpires ruled that pine tar on Brett's bat went too far up the handle and disallowed the homer. The league office had the final say, counting the home run and enabling the Royals to escape with a victory when the game was resumed later in the season.

Trivia Answer: Seven

JULY

25

Today's Trivia: On July 25, 1990, what comedian butchered the National Anthem in controversial fashion at a Reds-Padres game in San Diego?

Birthdays: Stanley Dancer, 1927; Nate Thurmond, 1941; Walter Payton, 1954; Doug Drabek, 1962; Ed Sprague, 1967; Billy Wagner, 1971; Guillermo Mota, 1973; Javier Vazquez, 1976; Kevin Kouzmanoff, 1981

On This Day: In 1976, Edwin Moses couldn't have picked a bigger setting to win his first international meet. Moses broke the world record and won the gold medal for the 400-meter hurdles at the Summer Olympics in Montreal.

Trivia Answer: Roseanne Barr

JULY

26

Today's Trivia: On July 26, 2010, Matt Garza threw the first no-hitter in the history of what Major League Baseball team?

Birthdays: Bob Waterfield, 1920; Hoyt Wilhelm, 1922; Tommy McDonald, 1934; Bob Lilly, 1939; Dorothy Hamill, 1956; Joe Smith, 1975; Brandon Morrow, 1984

On This Day: In 1952, Bob Mathias of the U.S. won the gold medal in the decathlon at the Summer Olympics in Helsinki. Having taken the gold at the 1948 Olympics, Mathias thus became the first person to win two straight gold medals in the history of the event.

Trivia Answer: Tampa Bay Rays

JULY

Today's Trivia: On July 27, 1993, the basketball world mourned the loss of what Celtics All-Star who collapsed on the court during an offseason workout?

Birthdays: Joe Tinker, 1880; Leo Durocher, 1905; Mack Calvin, 1947; Peggy Fleming, 1948; Marvin Barnes, 1952; Hugh Green, 1959; Shea Hillenbrand, 1975; Alex Rodriguez, 1975; Max Scherzer, 1984; Ryan Tannehill, 1988; Jordan Spieth, 1993

On This Day: In 1996, a pipe bomb exploded at Centennial Park in Atlanta during the Olympics. The blast claimed one life and injured over 100 more. Security guard Richard Jewell, who discovered the bomb, was considered a suspect, but never charged. Eric Robert Rudolph later confessed to the crime.

Trivia Answer: Reggie Lewis

JULY

Today's Trivia: On July 28, 1984, the Summer Games in Los Angeles officially began. What 1960 decathlon champion and film actor ignited the Olympic Flame during the opening ceremonies?

Birthdays: Bill Bradley, 1943; Vida Blue, 1949; Doug Collins, 1951; Dana White, 1969; Manu Ginobili, 1977; Chris Samuels, 1977; Julian Peterson, 1978; Zach Parise, 1984

On This Day: In 1991, Dennis Martinez pitched a perfect game as the Expos defeated the Dodgers, 2-0. It was the first by a Latin American player. Three years later to the day, Kenny Rogers was perfect as his Rangers beat the Angels, 4-0.

Trivia Answer: Rafer Johnson

JULY

Today's Trivia: On July 29, 1983, whose consecutive-game streak, which remains a National League record, came to an end at 1,207?

Birthdays: Ted Lindsay, 1925; Don Carter, 1926; Dan Driessen, 1951; Greg Minton, 1951; Scott Wedman, 1952; Ken Burns, 1953; Dirk Graham, 1959; Pepper Johnson, 1964; Luis Alicea, 1965; Sally Gunnel, 1966; Chad Billingsley, 1984

On This Day: In 1996, 35-year-old Carl Lewis leapt nearly 28 feet to win his fourth consecutive Olympic long jump. In doing so, he tied discus champion Al Oerter as the only Americans to win four straight gold medals in the same event. The medal was the final one of Lewis' legendary career.

Trivia Answer: Steve Garvey

JULY

Today's Trivia: On July 30, 1994, Michael Jordan hit his first home run as a professional baseball player. It came in his 354th at-bat, as a member of what Class AA minor league team?

Birthdays: Casey Stengel, 1890; Joe Nuxhall, 1928; Gus Triandos, 1930; Bud Selig, 1934; Jim Mandich, 1948; Bill Cartwright, 1957; Clint Hurdle, 1957; Tom Pagnozzi, 1962; Chris Mullin, 1963; Robert Porcher, 1969; Misty May-Treanor, 1977; Hope Solo, 1981

On This Day: In 1968, Washington Senators shortstop Ron Hansen turned in the first unassisted triple play in the Major Leagues in over 40 years. Hansen didn't fare as well at the plate, however, fanning four times against the Indians.

Trivia Answer: Birmingham Barons

JULY

Today's Trivia: On July 31, 2007, the Celtics completed their "Big Three" when Minnesota dealt them what star in the largest trade in NBA history for a single player?

Birthdays: Curt Gowdy, 1919; Hank Bauer, 1922; Norm Snead, 1939; Evonne Goolagong Cawley; 1951; Leon "Bull" Durham, 1957; Mark Cuban, 1958; Kevin Greene, 1962; Scott Bankhead, 1963; Chris Weinke, 1972; Jonathan Ogden, 1974; Gabe Kapler, 1975; Tim Couch, 1977; DeMarcus Ware, 1982; Evgeni Malkin, 1986; A.J. Green, 1988; Victoria Azarenka, 1989; Jose Fernandez, 1992

On This Day: In 1976, Sugar Ray Leonard was one of five U.S. boxers to win a gold medal at the Montreal Summer Olympics when he took down Cuba's Andres Aldama in the 139-pound weight class. Also winning the gold for the dominant Americans were Leon and Michael Spinks, Howard Davis and Leo Randolph.

Trivia Answer: Kevin Garnett (Five players and two picks were dealt for KG.)

AUGUST

Today's Trivia: On August 1, 1973, the ABA's Virginia Squires dealt what all-time great to the New York Nets, a team he'd lead to their only two championships?

Birthdays: Jack Kramer, 1921; Cliff Branch, 1948; Roy Williams, 1950; Kiki Vandeweghe, 1958; Greg Jefferies, 1967; Stacey Augmon, 1968; Shigetoshi Hasegawa, 1968; Edgerrin James, 1978; Adam Jones, 1985; Mike Wallace, 1986; Madison Bumgarner, 1989

On This Day: In 1996, Michael Johnson broke the world record in the 200 meters to win gold at the Summer Olympics in Atlanta. Three days earlier, Johnson won the 400 meters in record time, thus becoming the first man in history to win both events in one Olympics.

Trivia Answer: Julius Erving

AUGUST

Today's Trivia: On August 2, 1992, what track and field legend became the first woman ever to win two consecutive Olympic gold medals in the heptathlon?

Birthdays: Leo Boivin, 1932; Lamar Hunt, 1932; Billy Cannon, 1937; Tim Wakefield, 1966; Cedric Ceballos, 1969; Tony Amonte, 1970; Grady Sizemore, 1982; Huston Street, 1983; Golden Tate, 1988; Skylar Diggins, 1990; Laremy Tunsil, 1994; Kristaps Porzingis, 1995

On This Day: In 1979, Yankees catcher and team captain Thurman Munson died tragically at age 32. The private plane he was piloting crashed at Akron-Canton Airport in Ohio.

Trivia Answer: Jackie Joyner-Kersee

AUGUST

Today's Trivia: On August 3, 2000, the Pistons completed a trade to send superstar Grant Hill to a team he'd play just four games with the following season due to injury. Who?

Birthdays: Marv Levy, 1928; Lance Alworth, 1940; Marcel Dionne, 1951; Todd Christensen, 1956; Mike Gminski, 1959; Sid Bream, 1960; Rod Beck, 1968; Troy Glaus, 1976; Tom Brady, 1977; Matt Joyce, 1984; Ryan Lochte, 1984; Tyrod Taylor, 1989; Dante Fowler, Jr., 1994

On This Day: In 1986, the NFL redefined the word "football" in England. More than 80,000 people jammed London's Wembley Stadium for the first "American Bowl" to watch an exhibition game between the defending champion Chicago Bears and the Dallas Cowboys. The Bears won, 17-6.

Trivia Answer: Orlando Magic

AUGUST

Today's Trivia: On August 4, 1993, a bench-clearing brawl ensued when Nolan Ryan infamously put what White Sox All-Star in a headlock after he charged the mound from a Ryan beaning?

Birthdays: Maurice "Rocket" Richard, 1921; Dallas Green, 1934; Cleon Jones, 1942; John Riggins, 1949; Mary Decker Slaney, 1958; Roger Clemens, 1962; John Farrell, 1962; B.J. Surhoff, 1964; Jeff Gordon, 1971; Eric Milton, 1975

On This Day: In 1982, Joel Youngblood became the first Major Leaguer to get a hit for two different teams in two different cities on the same day. In the afternoon in Chicago, the Mets All-Star singled in two runs against the Cubs and Ferguson Jenkins. That evening in Philadelphia, he donned an Expos uniform in time to hit another single off the Phillies' Steve Carlton.

Trivia Answer: Robin Ventura

AUGUST

Today's Trivia: On August 5, 1967, who became the first African-American to be inducted into the Pro Football Hall of Fame?

Birthdays: Herb Brooks, 1937; Roman Gabriel, 1940; Patrick Ewing, 1962; Otis Thorpe, 1962; John Olerud, 1968; Eric Hinske, 1977; Mark Mulder, 1977; Carl Crawford, 1981; Lolo Jones, 1982; Paula Creamer, 1986

On This Day: In 1936, Jesse Owens edged out fellow American Mack Robinson to capture the gold in the 200-meter dash at the Summer Olympics in Berlin. It was Owens' third of four gold medals at the Germany Games - an embarrassment to the host, Aryan-supremacist Adolf Hitler.

Trivia Answer: Emlen Tunnell

AUGUST

Today's Trivia: On August 6, 1952, what 46-year-old became the oldest MLB pitcher to hurl a complete game shutout in a St. Louis Browns win over the Tigers?

Birthdays: Henry Iba, 1904; Clem Labine, 1926; Andy Messersmith, 1945; Bob Horner, 1957; Dale Ellis, 1960; David Robinson, 1965; Mike Budenholzer, 1969; Wilmer Flores, 1991

On This Day: In 1926, Gertrude Ederle became the first woman to swim across the English Channel. A three-time medalist at the 1924 Olympics, Ederle swam the 21 miles separating Great Britain from the northwestern tip of France in 14 and a half hours.

Trivia Answer: Satchel Paige, with a 1-0, 12-inning victory

AUGUST

Today's Trivia: On August 7, 1999, who became the first player in MLB history to hit a home run for his 3,000th hit?

Birthdays: Bobby Doerr, 1918; Don Larsen, 1929; Carlos Monzon, 1942; Alan Page, 1945; Jason Grimsley, 1967; Danny Graves, 1973; Shane Lechler, 1976; Edgar Renteria, 1976; Sidney Crosby, 1987; Jordan Cameron, 1988; DeMar DeRozan, 1989; Mike Trout, 1991

On This Day: In 2007, Barry Bonds hit home run #756 off a pitch from Mike Bacsik of the Nationals, breaking the all-time record of Hank Aaron. Bonds would finish his career with 762 homers.

Trivia Answer: Wade Boggs

AUGUST

Today's Trivia: On August 8, 1992, the U.S. men's basketball team, featuring NBA players for the first time, cruised to gold at the Barcelona Olympics. Who did they defeat?

Birthdays: Johnny Temple, 1927; Frank Howard, 1936; Jose Cruz, 1947; Ken Dryden, 1947; Brian Sipe, 1949; Nigel Mansell, 1953; Bruce Matthews, 1961; Rashard Lewis, 1979; Roger Federer, 1981; Pierre Garcon, 1986; Danilo Gallinari, 1988; Anthony Rizzo, 1989

On This Day: In 1988, the lights came on in Chicago as the Phillies and the Cubs met in the first-ever night game at Wrigley Field. Twelve years earlier to the day, the "lites" came out at Comiskey Park as the White Sox wore new "lite" uniforms featuring Bermuda shorts. Thankfully, the new look was short-lived.

Trivia Answer: Croatia, 117-85

AUGUST

Today's Trivia: On August 9, 2012, who became the first man to win the 100 and 200-meter races in consecutive Olympics?

Birthdays: Bob Cousy, 1928; Rod Laver, 1938; Tommie Agee, 1942; Ken Norton, 1943; Jim Kiick, 1946; Ted Simmons, 1949; Doug Williams, 1955; Louis Lipps, 1962; Hot Rod Williams, 1962; Brett Hull, 1964; John Smith, 1965; Deion Sanders, 1967; Troy Percival, 1969; Derek Fisher, 1974; Matt Morris, 1974; Brian Fuentes, 1975; Chamique Holdsclaw, 1977; Adewale Ogunleye, 1977; Tyson Gay, 1982; JaMarcus Russell, 1985; Jason Heyward, 1989

On This Day: In 1988, the Edmonton Oilers shocked the hockey world by trading superstar Wayne Gretzky to the Los Angeles Kings. In exchange, the Oilers received two players, three draft picks and $15 million in cash.

Trivia Answer: Usain Bolt

AUGUST 10

Today's Trivia: On August 10, 1984, what heavily favored U.S. runner's quest for gold in the 3000 meters literally came crashing down when she got tangled up with Zola Budd?

Birthdays: Red Holzman, 1920, Rocky Colavito, 1933; John Starks, 1965; Gerald Williams, 1966; Riddick Bowe, 1967; Samari Rolle, 1976; Wilson Ramos, 1987; Anthony Gose, 1990; Archie Bradley, 1992; Andre Drummond, 1993

On This Day: In 1971, Harmon Killebrew hit the 500th home run of his career. Exactly ten years later, Pete Rose recorded hit #3,631, breaking the National League all-time mark set by Stan Musial.

Trivia Answer: Mary Decker

AUGUST 11

Today's Trivia: On August 11, 1991, what 25-year-old unknown and ninth alternate for the tournament stunned the golf world by winning the PGA Championship?

Birthdays: Bill Monbouquette, 1936; Vada Pinson, 1938; Otis Taylor, 1942; Bryn Smith, 1955; Craig Ehlo, 1961; Melky Cabrera, 1984; Colby Rasmus, 1986; Pablo Sandoval, 1986; Drew Storen, 1987

On This Day: In 1984, Carl Lewis finished off a remarkable Olympic run with a record performance in the men's 400-meter relay. In claiming his fourth gold medal at the L.A. Games, he matched Jesse Owens' historic mark set in 1936.

Trivia Answer: John Daly

AUGUST

12

Today's Trivia: On August 12, 1978, the career of what promising Patriots receiver came to an abrupt end when he was paralyzed after a hit in a preseason game from Oakland's Jack Tatum?

Birthdays: Christy Mathewson, 1880; Fred Hutchinson, 1919; George McGinnis, 1950; Lynette Woodard, 1959; Pete Sampras, 1971; Matt Clement, 1974; Antoine Walker, 1976; Plaxico Burress, 1977; Delanie Walker, 1984; Jose Tabata, 1988; Khris Middleton, 1991; Chris Owings, 1991

On This Day: In 1994, Major League Baseball players went on strike. The result would be the cancellation of the World Series for the first time in 90 years, as baseball became the first sport in history to lose its postseason to a labor dispute. The work stoppage was the eighth in baseball history.

Trivia Answer: Darryl Stingley

AUGUST

13

Today's Trivia: On August 13, 1999, two months removed from her French Open title, what great announced her retirement from tennis at the age of 30?

Birthdays: Ben Hogan, 1912; Mudcat Grant, 1935; Tony Cloninger, 1940; Bobby Clarke, 1949; Betsy King, 1955; Jay Buhner, 1964; Mark Lemke, 1965; Elvis Grbac, 1970; Jarrod Washburn, 1974; Marty Turco, 1975; Corey Patterson, 1979; Dallas Braden, 1983; DeMarcus Cousins, 1990; Johnny Gaudreau, 1993

On This Day: In 1919, horse racing legend Man o' War suffered his only defeat in 21 races, at the Sanford Memorial Stakes in Saratoga, NY. The horse that beat him was appropriately named Upset.

Trivia Answer: Steffi Graf

AUGUST 14

Today's Trivia: On August 14, 1987, whose 39th homer of the season set a new MLB record for home runs by a rookie?

Birthdays: Wellington Mara, 1916; Dick Tiger, 1929; Earl Weaver, 1930; John Brodie, 1935; Debbie Meyer, 1952; Mark Fidrych, 1954; Rusty Wallace, 1956; Magic Johnson, 1959; Mark Gubicza, 1962; Neal Anderson, 1964; Mark Loretta, 1971; Wayne Chrebet, 1973; Mike Vrabel, 1975; Juan Pierre, 1977; Roy Williams, 1980; Clay Buchholz, 1984; Shea Weber, 1985; Tim Tebow, 1987; Kiko Alonso, 1990

On This Day: In 1977, Lanny Wadkins won the PGA Championship in the first-ever sudden-death playoff in a stroke-play major championship. Wadkins claimed his lone major by defeating Gene Littler on the third hole of the playoff.

Trivia Answer: Mark McGwire (He finished the year with 49.)

AUGUST 15

Today's Trivia: On August 15, 1993, Paul Azinger won his only major when he prevailed in a sudden-death playoff at the PGA Championship. The golfer he defeated joined Craig Wood as the only men to lose playoffs in all four major championships. Who?

Birthdays: Charlie Comiskey, 1859; Lionel Taylor, 1935; Gene Upshaw, 1945; Sam Cunningham, 1950; Craig MacTavish, 1958; Gary Kubiak, 1961; Scott Brosius, 1966; Yancey Thigpen, 1969; Kerri Walsh Jennings, 1978; Carl Edwards, 1979; Oliver Perez, 1981

On This Day: In 2005, 19-year-old Felix Hernandez became the first teenager to strike out 10 or more batters in one game since Dwight Gooden, fanning 11 Royals. Exactly seven years later, King Felix threw the 23rd perfect game in MLB history, a 1-0 win over Tampa Bay.

Trivia Answer: Greg Norman

The Bathroom Sports Almanac

AUGUST

Today's Trivia: On August 16, 1954, the very first issue of *Sports Illustrated* was published. What Milwaukee Braves star was shown at the plate on the inaugural cover?

Birthdays: Amos Alonzo Stagg, 1862; Frank Gifford, 1930; Tony Trabert, 1930; Ron Yary, 1946; Christian Okoye, 1961; Rick Reed, 1964; Ben Coates, 1969; Quinton McCracken, 1970; Kevin Williams, 1980; Yu Darvish, 1986; Carey Price, 1987

On This Day: In 1920, at the Polo Grounds, Ray Chapman suffered a fractured skull and died the next day as a result of being hit by a wild pitch from Yankee pitcher Carl Mays. The Indian shortstop is the only on-field player fatality in Major League Baseball history.

Trivia Answer: Ed Mathews

AUGUST

Today's Trivia: On August 17, 1973, who hit the 660th and final home run of his Major League career?

Birthdays: Boog Powell, 1941; Guillermo Vilas, 1952; Dottie Mochrie, 1965; Jon Gruden, 1963; Ed McCaffrey, 1968; Christian Laettner, 1969; Jim Courier, 1970; Jorge Posada, 1971; Mike Maroth, 1977; Antwaan Randle El, 1979; Brett Myers, 1980; Dustin Pedroia, 1983; Rudy Gay, 1986; Gracie Gold, 1995

On This Day: In 2008, Michael Phelps won his eighth gold medal at the Beijing Summer Games, breaking Mark Spitz's record for the most golds in a single Olympics. The mark was set in the 4×100-meter medley relay. Phelps, along with Brendan Hansen, Aaron Peirsol, and Jason Lezak, set a new world record in the event.

Trivia Answer: Willie Mays

AUGUST

Today's Trivia: On August 18, 2009, Brett Favre made his final NFL stop, signing on with what team?

Birthdays: Burleigh Grimes, 1893; Roberto Clemente, 1934; Rafer Johnson, 1935; Matt Snell, 1941; Greg Pruitt, 1951; Bruce Benedict, 1955; Lafayette "Fat" Lever, 1960; Brian Mitchell, 1968; Bobby Higginson, 1970; Adalius Thomas, 1977; Bart Scott, 1980; Jeremy Shockey, 1980; Dontari Poe, 1990; Willie Cauley-Stein, 1993

On This Day: In 1992, Boston Celtics forward Larry Bird announced his retirement from the game at age 35. Bird, along with Magic Johnson, was credited with reviving the slumbering NBA. His retirement came six years to the day after a fellow Rookie of the Year and MVP, Earl Campbell, said goodbye to the game of football.

Trivia Answer: Minnesota Vikings

AUGUST

Today's Trivia: On August 19, 1921, what 34-year-old, who remains the youngest to ever reach the mark, recorded the 3,000th hit of his MLB career?

Birthdays: Bill Shoemaker, 1931; Bobby Richardson, 1935; Al Oerter, 1936; Ned Yost, 1954; Gary Gaetti, 1958; Anthony Munoz, 1958; Ricky Pierce, 1959; Morten Andersen, 1960; Ron Darling, 1960; Bobby Hebert, 1960; Woody Williams, 1966; Mary Joe Fernandez, 1971; Chris Capuano, 1978; Thomas Jones, 1978; J.J. Hardy, 1982; Kirk Cousins, 1988

On This Day: In 1951, three-foot, seven-inch Eddie Gaedel pinch-hit for the St. Louis Browns against the Detroit Tigers. Wearing the number "1/8," Gaedel, a brainchild of owner Bill Veeck, walked on four pitches. American League president Will Harridge, claiming Veeck was making a mockery of the game, voided Gaedel's contract the next day.

Trivia Answer: Ty Cobb

AUGUST

20

Today's Trivia: On August 20, 1955, three years before he won his first of seven majors, who scored his first career win on the PGA Tour when he captured the Canadian Open?

Birthdays: Al Lopez, 1908; Don King, 1931; Si Green, 1933; Graig Nettles, 1944; Tom Brunansky, 1960; Mark Langston, 1960; Andy Benes, 1967; Todd Helton, 1973

On This Day: In 1974, Nolan Ryan struck out 19 batters, but lost, 1-0, in 11 innings to Detroit's Mickey Lolich. It marked the third time that season that Ryan had fanned 19.

Trivia Answer: Arnold Palmer

AUGUST

21

Today's Trivia: On August 21, 1947, what inaugural event, which would be won by the Maynard Midgets, took place in Williamsport, Pennsylvania?

Birthdays: Toe Blake, 1912; Chris Schenkel, 1923; Jack Buck, 1924; Wilt Chamberlain, 1936; Felix Millan, 1943; Willie Lanier, 1945; John Stearns, 1951; Archie Griffin, 1954; Jim McMahon, 1959; John Wetteland, 1966; Craig Counsell, 1970; Jason Marquis, 1978; B.J. Upton, 1984; Usain Bolt, 1986; J.D. Martinez, 1987; Mike Evans, 1993

On This Day: In 2013, Yankees outfielder Ichiro Suzuki recorded his 4,000th career hit as a professional baseball player, a single off of Toronto's R.A. Dickey. Ichiro collected 1,278 hits in Japan before his Major League Baseball career began with Seattle in 2001.

Trivia Answer: Little League World Series

AUGUST

22

Today's Trivia: On August 22, 2007, who became the first team in modern MLB history to score 30 runs in a game when they destroyed the Orioles, 30-3?

Birthdays: Carl Yastrzemski, 1939; Bill Parcells, 1941; Paul Molitor, 1956; Mats Wilander, 1964; Jeff Weaver, 1976; Randy Wolf, 1976; Jahri Evans, 1983; Mohamed Sanu, 1989; Randall Cobb, 1990; Drew Hutchison, 1990

On This Day: In 1851, the first international yacht race took place, in the English Channel off the Isle of Wight. The sole U.S. entry, the America, outdistanced over a dozen other boats in the event that is now known as the America's Cup.

Trivia Answer: Texas Rangers

AUGUST

23

Today's Trivia: On August 23, 1987, what Brazilian basketball star poured in 46 points to lead his country to a stunning victory over the U.S. in the title match of the Pan American Games?

Birthdays: George Kell, 1922; Sonny Jurgensen, 1934; Mike Boddicker, 1957; Julio Franco, 1958; Rik Smits, 1966; Cortez Kennedy, 1968; Hugh Douglas, 1971; Kobe Bryant, 1978; Rex Grossman, 1980; Natalie Coughlin, 1982; Jeremy Lin, 1988

On This Day: In 1936, a 17-year-old pitcher named Bob Feller made his first MLB start for the Cleveland Indians. The young right-hander struck out 15 while allowing only six hits in a 4-1 complete game victory over the St. Louis Browns.

Trivia Answer: Oscar Schmidt

AUGUST

Today's Trivia: On August 24, 1988, what North Stars All-Star was sentenced to a day in jail for hitting another player in the head with his hockey stick during a game earlier in the year?

Birthdays: Mike Shanahan, 1952; Cal Ripken, Jr., 1960; Reggie Miller, 1965; Tim Salmon, 1968; Michael Redd, 1979; Brett Gardner, 1983; Arian Foster, 1986; Anze Kopitar, 1987; Allen Robinson, 1993

On This Day: In 1989, Commissioner Bart Giamatti announced a permanent banishment from baseball for Pete Rose. Rose had bet on Major League Baseball games, including ones he was a part of as the manager of the Cincinnati Reds. He remains absent from the Hall of Fame.

Trivia Answer: Dino Ciccarelli

AUGUST

Today's Trivia: On August 25, 1985, what 20-year-old became the youngest pitcher in MLB history to win 20 games in a season?

Birthdays: Althea Gibson, 1927; Rollie Fingers, 1946; Cornelius Bennett, 1965; Albert Belle, 1966; Doug Glanville, 1970; Robert Horry, 1970; Marvin Harrison, 1972; Gary Matthews, Jr., 1974; Pedro Feliciano, 1976; Logan Morrison, 1987; Justin Upton, 1987

On This Day: In 1996, 20-year-old Stanford student Tiger Woods came from behind to defeat Steve Scott and win his third consecutive U.S. Amateur title. Woods would turn pro a few days later.

Trivia Answer: Dwight Gooden, when his Mets beat the Padres

AUGUST

26

Today's Trivia: On August 26, 1996, the Tampa Bay Storm defeated the Iowa Barnstormers, 42-38, in Arena Bowl X. Future NFL head coach Jay Gruden quarterbacked the Storm, while what future NFL MVP was behind center for Iowa?

Birthdays: Tom Heinsohn, 1934; Swede Savage, 1946; Donnie Shell, 1952; Stan Van Gundy, 1959; Roger Kingdom, 1962; Ricky Bottalico, 1969; Morgan Ensberg, 1975; Kyle Kendrick, 1984; David Price, 1985; Elvis Andrus, 1988; James Harden, 1989

On This Day: In 1939, a Major League Baseball game was televised for the first time. New York station W2XBS broadcast a doubleheader between the Reds and Dodgers at Ebbets Field. Red Barber called the game from a perch amid the fans in the upper deck.

Trivia Answer: Kurt Warner

AUGUST

27

Today's Trivia: On August 27, 2004, the U.S. men's basketball team suffered a disappointing loss in their semifinal game in Athens. What gold medal winners took them down?

Birthdays: Frank Leahy, 1908; Joe Cunningham, 1931; Buddy Bell, 1951; Mack Brown, 1951; Bernhard Langer, 1957; Adam Oates, 1962; Michael Dean Perry, 1965; Brian McRae, 1967; Jim Thome, 1970; Jose Vidro, 1974; Rashean Mathis, 1980; Darren McFadden, 1987; Breanna Stewart, 1994

On This Day: In 1982, Rickey Henderson stole his 119th base of the year, breaking the record set by Lou Brock in 1974. Henderson finished the game with four steals, and would end the season with 130.

Trivia Answer: Argentina

AUGUST

Today's Trivia: On August 28, 1922, what inaugural golf match, in which the U.S. defeated Great Britain & Ireland, 8-4, got underway?

Birthdays: Andy Bathgate, 1932; Lou Piniella, 1943; Mike Torrez, 1946; Ron Guidry, 1950; Joel Youngblood, 1951; Scott Hamilton, 1958; Pierre Turgeon, 1969; Janet Evans, 1971; Ryan Madson, 1980; Carlos Quentin, 1982; Gerry McNamara, 1983; Nate Washington, 1983; Jeff Green, 1986

On This Day: In 1977, Brazilian soccer legend Pele played his final North American Soccer League game, leading the New York Cosmos to the championship. A few years earlier, Pele had signed a $7 million contract, making him the highest paid athlete in the world.

Trivia Answer: The Walker Cup

AUGUST

Today's Trivia: On August 29, 1974, who became the first player to go directly from high school to pro basketball when he signed with the ABA's Utah Stars?

Birthdays: Wyomia Tyus, 1945; Bob Beamon, 1946; Jerry Bailey, 1957; Rodney McCray, 1961; Carl Banks, 1962; Henry Blanco, 1971; Roy Oswalt, 1977; Aaron Rowand, 1977; Jamal Lewis, 1979; David West, 1980; Leon Washington, 1982; Marc Rzepczynski, 1985; Noah Syndergaard, 1992

On This Day: In 1972, in a 3-0 victory, Giants right-hander Jim Barr retired the first 20 Cardinals he faced. That gave him a Major League record of 41 consecutive outs as he'd retired the last 21 in his previous start. The current record for consecutive batters retired is 46, set by another Giant, reliever Yusmeiro Petit.

Trivia Answer: Moses Malone

AUGUST

30

Today's Trivia: On August 30, 1978, what Japanese baseball player hit his 800th career home run?

Birthdays: Ted Williams, 1918; Jerry Tarkanian, 1930; Coy Bacon, 1942; Jean-Claude Killy, 1943; Tug McGraw, 1944; Robert Parish, 1953; Shaun Alexander, 1977; Marlon Byrd, 1977; Cliff Lee, 1978; Roberto Hernandez, 1980; Adam Wainwright, 1981; Andy Roddick, 1982; Joe Staley, 1984; Duane Brown, 1985

On This Day: In 1991, Mike Powell broke a long-standing record when he jumped 29 feet, 4.5 inches in the long jump at the World Track and Field Championships in Tokyo. Powell's leap topped the mark set by Bob Beamon at the 1968 Summer Olympics.

Trivia Answer: Sadaharu Oh

AUGUST

31

Today's Trivia: On August 31, 2001, Dominican officials confirmed that what player was too old to compete after he had just led his Bronx team to a third-place finish in the Little League World Series?

Birthdays: Jim Finks, 1927; Jean Beliveau, 1931; Frank Robinson, 1935; Tom Coughlin, 1946; Claudell Washington, 1954; Edwin Moses, 1955; Tom Candiotti, 1957; Hideo Nomo, 1968; Larry Fitzgerald, 1983; Ted Ligety, 1984; Matt Adams, 1988

On This Day: In 1990, Ken Griffey and Ken Griffey, Jr., made history when they played together on the same Major League team, the Seattle Mariners. And it was "like father, like son," as they each singled in the first inning.

Trivia Answer: Danny Almonte

SEPTEMBER

Today's Trivia: On September 1, 2007, what team stunned the college football world with a 34-32 season opening win over the Michigan Wolverines?

Birthdays: Gentleman Jim Corbett, 1866; Woody Stephens, 1913; Rocky Marciano, 1923; Guy Rodgers, 1935; Al Geiberger, 1937; Vinnie Johnson, 1956; Karl Mecklenburg, 1960; Hardy Nickerson, 1965; Tim Hardaway, 1966; Zach Thomas, 1973; Jason Taylor, 1974; Clinton Portis, 1981; Calais Campbell, 1986

On This Day: In 1946, Patty Berg won the first U.S. Women's Open by defeating Betty Jameson. Berg, a founding member of the LPGA Tour, would go on to win 15 majors in her career, the most of any female golfer.

Trivia Answer: Appalachian State Mountaineers

SEPTEMBER

Today's Trivia: On September 2, 1991, what 39-year-old tennis great scored an improbable fourth round U.S. Open win after entering the tournament as an afterthought?

Birthdays: Albert Spalding, 1850; Adolph Rupp, 1901; D. Wayne Lukas, 1935; Peter Ueberroth, 1937; John Thompson, 1941; Glen Sather, 1943; Terry Bradshaw, 1948; Nate "Tiny" Archibald, 1948; Jimmy Connors, 1952; Eric Dickerson, 1960; Lennox Lewis, 1965; Rich Aurilia, 1971; Brian Westbrook, 1979; Gaby Sanchez, 1983; Marcus & Markieff Morris, 1989; Brandon Ingram, 1997

On This Day: In 1972, Milt Pappas of the Cubs was one strike away from perfection before he threw two straight balls and walked the only batter who would reach base in the game. He settled for a no-hitter. Exactly 29 years later, New York's Mike Mussina would lose his perfect game with two outs and two strikes in the bottom of the ninth vs. Boston. He would settle for his fourth career one-hitter.

Trivia Answer: Jimmy Connors (He would lose to Jim Courier in the semis.)

SEPTEMBER

Today's Trivia: On September 3, 1995, what two new NFL franchises played their very first regular season contests?

Birthdays: Eddie Stanky, 1916; Bennie Blades, 1966; Luis Gonzalez, 1967; Damon Stoudamire, 1973; Jevon Kearse, 1976; Casey Hampton, 1977; Nate Robertson, 1977; Jennie Finch, 1980; Shaun White, 1986; Domonic Brown, 1987

On This Day: In 1970, the football world lost one of its most legendary figures when Vince Lombardi died at 57 years old. Lombardi, who won five championships in a seven-year period with the Packers, never had a losing season coaching in the NFL.

Trivia Answer: Jacksonville Jaguars and Carolina Panthers (Both lost.)

SEPTEMBER

Today's Trivia: On September 4, 1993, the Yankees defeated the Indians, 4-0, as what pitcher threw one of the most memorable no-hitters in MLB history?

Birthdays: Ken Harrelson, 1941; Raymond Floyd, 1942; Tom Watson, 1949; Frank White, 1950; Shane Gould, 1956; John Vanbiesbrouck, 1963; Mike Piazza, 1968; Terence Newman, 1978; Andrelton Simmons, 1989

On This Day: In 1972, Mark Spitz swam the fly leg of the 400-meter medley relay to win his seventh gold medal of the Munich Summer Games. Before Spitz, no one had won more than five gold medals in an Olympics. His record, of course, would later be broken by a fellow swimmer.

Trivia Answer: Jim Abbott

SEPTEMBER

5

Today's Trivia: On September 5, 1979, who became the first and only woman to sign a contract with an NBA team, the Indiana Pacers?

Birthdays: Nap Lajoie, 1874; Bill Mazeroski, 1936; Billy Kilmer, 1939; Willie Gault, 1960; Candy Maldonado, 1960; Jeff Brantley, 1963; Dennis Scott, 1968; Rod Barajas, 1975; Stacey Dales, 1979; Chris Young, 1983; Colt McCoy, 1986; Elena Delle Donne, 1989; Lance Stephenson, 1990

On This Day: In 1972, Palestinian terrorists broke into the Olympic Village in Munich and took a group of Israeli athletes hostage for the avowed purpose of freeing Arab guerrillas held in Israeli prisons. Eleven Israeli team members and five of the terrorists were killed.

Trivia Answer: Ann Meyers

SEPTEMBER

6

Today's Trivia: On September 6, 1976, what 21-year-old won her second-straight U.S. Open two years to the day after having a record streak of 55 consecutive match wins snapped?

Birthdays: Vince DiMaggio, 1912; Hal Jeffcoat, 1924; Dow Finsterwald, 1929; Ron Boone, 1946; Kevin Willis, 1962; Tim Henman, 1974; Derrek Lee, 1975; Ryan Clady, 1986; John Wall, 1990

On This Day: In 1995, Cal Ripken, Jr. played in his 2,131st consecutive game, breaking Lou Gehrig's record. In the fourth inning, Ripken sent the Baltimore fans into a frenzy when he hit his 15th home run of the season. When the game became official after the top of the fifth, Ripken received a standing ovation that lasted over 20 minutes.

Trivia Answer: Chris Evert

SEPTEMBER

Today's Trivia: On September 7, 1993, what Cardinals outfielder tied two MLB records when he hit four home runs and drove in 12 runs in a single game vs. the Reds?

Birthdays: Paul Brown, 1908; Louise Suggs, 1923; Al McGuire, 1928; Clyde Lovellette, 1929; Jacques Lemaire, 1945; Bert Jones, 1951; Bruce Armstrong, 1965; "Sugar" Shane Mosley, 1971; Jason Isringhausen, 1972; Antonio McDyess, 1974; Mark Prior, 1980; Wade Davis, 1985; Kevin Love, 1988

On This Day: In 1979, the Entertainment and Sports Programming Network made its debut. An estimated 30,000 viewers tuned in to ESPN for the first *SportsCenter* telecast with anchors Lee Leonard and George Grande. Said Leonard to viewers, "If you love sports...you'll think you've died and gone to sports heaven."

Trivia Answer: Mark Whiten

SEPTEMBER

Today's Trivia: On September 8, 1965, what A's shortstop became the first player to play every position in a single Major League game?

Birthdays: Lem Barney, 1945; Rogie Vachon, 1945; Ken Forsch, 1946; L.C. Greenwood, 1946; Maurice Cheeks, 1956; Latrell Sprewell, 1970; Amani Toomer, 1974; Gil Meche, 1978; Malcom Floyd, 1981; Matt Barkley, 1990; Gerrit Cole, 1990; Matthew Dellavedova, 1990; Tyler Eifert, 1990

On This Day: In 1998, Mark McGwire passed Roger Maris with his 62nd home run of the season. Playing against Sammy Sosa and the Cubs, McGwire lined a Steve Trachsel pitch over the left field wall for the record breaker. Big Mac would finish the year with 70 homers, a mark which would be topped by Barry Bonds, who hit 73 in 2001.

Trivia Answer: Bert Campaneris

SEPTEMBER

Today's Trivia: On September 9, 1965, what southpaw threw the first perfect game of his career, which doubled as his fourth no-hitter?

Birthdays: Frank Chance, 1876; Frankie Frisch, 1897; Waite Hoyt, 1899; Dick LeBeau, 1937; Lem Barney, 1945; Joe Theismann, 1949; Walter Davis, 1954; Bob Stoops, 1960; Alvin Davis, 1960; Dan Majerle, 1965; Todd Zeile, 1965; B.J. Armstrong, 1967; Mike Hampton, 1972; Shane Battier, 1978; Edwin Jackson, 1983; J.R. Smith, 1985

On This Day: In 1972, the U.S. men's basketball team's 63-game Olympic winning streak came to a controversial end when they lost to the Soviet Union, 51-50, in the gold medal contest in Munich. Because of issues with the game clock and horn going off, the Soviets were given three chances to convert a last-second inbound pass for the winning bucket.

Trivia Answer: Sandy Koufax

SEPTEMBER

Today's Trivia: On September 10, 1989, what Colt became the fastest player ever to reach 10,000 yards rushing?

Birthdays: Ted Kluszewski, 1924; Arnold Palmer, 1929; Roger Maris, 1934; Buck Buchanan, 1940; Bob Lanier, 1948; Randy Johnson, 1963; Ben Wallace, 1974; Gustavo Kuerten, 1976; Jay Williams, 1981; Joey Votto, 1983; Neil Walker, 1985; Paul Goldschmidt, 1987

On This Day: In 1989, Deion Sanders returned a punt 68 yards for a touchdown in his NFL debut with the Atlanta Falcons. Five days earlier, Sanders hit a home run as a New York Yankee. "Prime Time" remains the only athlete to play in both a Super Bowl (with the Cowboys and 49ers) and World Series (with the Braves).

Trivia Answer: Eric Dickerson

SEPTEMBER

Today's Trivia: On September 11, 1918, what team defeated the Cubs in six games to win their last World Series of the century?

Birthdays: Paul "Bear" Bryant, 1913; Tom Landry, 1924; Franz Beckenbauer, 1945; Lesley Visser, 1953; Don Slaught, 1958; Gerald Wilkins, 1963; Ellis Burks, 1964; Eduardo Perez, 1969; Ed Reed, 1978; Jacoby Ellsbury, 1983; Mike Moustakas, 1988

On This Day: In 1985, Cincinnati's Pete Rose singled off Eric Show to become Major League Baseball's all-time hits leader. Rose passed Ty Cobb to top the list with 4,192. When Rose retired, he left a new mark of 4,256 hits.

Trivia Answer: Boston Red Sox

SEPTEMBER

Today's Trivia: On September 12, 2004, with a win at Chicago, what team snapped the longest road losing streak in NFL history at 24 games?

Birthdays: Jesse Owens, 1913; Charlie Keller, 1916; Glenn A. Davis, 1934; Mickey Lolich, 1940; John "Frenchy" Fuqua, 1946; Vernon Maxwell, 1965; Pat Listach, 1967, Ki-Jana Carter, 1973; Luis Castillo, 1975; Sean Burroughs, 1980; Yao Ming, 1980; Freddie Freeman, 1989; Andrew Luck, 1989

On This Day: In 1962, Washington's Tom Cheney, after finishing the first nine innings with "just" 13 Ks, went on to strike out a record 21 batters in a 16-inning, 2-1 win vs. Baltimore.

Trivia Answer: Detroit Lions

SEPTEMBER

13

Today's Trivia: On September 13, 2015, what 18-year-old became the youngest woman ever to win a major championship when she claimed the Evian Championship in France?

Birthdays: Emile Francis, 1926; Rick Wise, 1945; Michael Johnson, 1967; Brad Johnson, 1968; Denny Neagle, 1968; Bernie Williams, 1968; Goran Ivanisevic, 1971; Daisuke Matsuzaka, 1980; Nene, 1982; Rickie Weeks, 1982

On This Day: In 1989, Fay Vincent was named Commissioner of Major League Baseball, replacing Bart Giamatti, who died suddenly on September 1 of a heart attack. In other baseball news, this date in 1965 and '71 marked the 500th home runs in the respective careers of Willie Mays and Frank Robinson.

Trivia Answer: Lydia Ko

SEPTEMBER

14

Today's Trivia: On September 14, 1968, who won his 30th game of the season, becoming the last MLB pitcher to date to do so?

Birthdays: Jerry Coleman, 1924; Harry Sinden, 1932; Larry Brown, 1940; Tim Wallach, 1957; Delmon Young, 1985; Michael Crabtree, 1987; Jimmy Butler, 1989

On This Day: In 1923, Jack Dempsey knocked out Luis Firpo one minute into the second round to retain his heavyweight title. There were a dozen knockdowns in the fight with Firpo hitting the canvas ten times. Exactly 45 years later, Jimmy Ellis took down Floyd Patterson in a much longer fight, a controversial 15 round decision, to claim the heavyweight title.

Trivia Answer: Denny McLain

SEPTEMBER

Today's Trivia: On September 15, 1978, what 36-year-old became the first boxer to win the world heavyweight title three times when he defeated Leon Spinks?

Birthdays: Gaylord Perry, 1938; Merlin Olsen, 1940; Pete Carroll, 1951; Joel Quenneville, 1958; Joe Morris, 1960; Dan Marino, 1961; Will Shields, 1971; Jason Terry, 1977; Patrick Marleau, 1979; Mike Dunleavy, Jr., 1980; Luke Hochevar, 1983; Marshal Yanda, 1984

On This Day: In 1969, Steve Carlton became the first pitcher in the 20th century to strike out 19 batters in a nine-inning game - but lost anyway. Carlton fanned everyone in the Mets starting lineup at least once, but Ron Swoboda hit two homers to defeat the Cardinals, 4-3.

Trivia Answer: Muhammad Ali

SEPTEMBER

Today's Trivia: On September 16, 1975, who made history by going seven-for-seven in one game when his Pirates routed the Cubs, 22-0?

Birthdays: Elgin Baylor, 1934; Larry Grantham, 1938; Dennis Connor, 1942; Robin Yount, 1955; Orel Hershiser, 1958; Tim Raines, 1959; Mickey Tettleton, 1960; Brandon Moss, 1983; Matt Harrison, 1985

On This Day: In 1993, Dave Winfield collected hit #3,000 off of A's pitcher Dennis Eckersley. Exactly three years later, another Twin, Paul Molitor, recorded his 3,000th. Fast forward another 11 years to the day, in 2007, Chicago's Jim Thome (a future Twin) hit a walk-off shot for his 500th career home run.

Trivia Answer: Rennie Stennett

SEPTEMBER

17

Today's Trivia: On September 17, 1961, Fran
Tarkenton threw four touchdown passes in his very first
NFL game for what team that was also making its pro football
debut?

Birthdays: George Blanda, 1927; Stirling Moss, 1929;
Maureen Connolly, 1934; Orlando Cepeda, 1937; Phil Jackson,
1945; Anthony Carter, 1960; John Franco, 1960; Mark Brunell, 1970;
Rasheed Wallace, 1974; Jimmie Johnson, 1975; Dan Haren, 1980;
Alexander Ovechkin, 1985

On This Day: In 1912, Brooklyn centerfielder Casey Stengel
made an impressive Major League debut as he collected four singles
and a pair of stolen bases. Exactly 29 years later, Stan Musial made
his MLB debut for the Cardinals, going 2-for-4 with a pair of RBIs.

Trivia Answer: Minnesota Vikings (They defeated the Chicago Bears.)

SEPTEMBER

18

Today's Trivia: On September 18, 1963, the
Phillies beat the Mets, 5-1, in the final MLB game played
at what historic park?

Birthdays: Harvey Haddix, 1925; Bud Greenspan, 1926;
Scotty Bowman, 1933; Darryl Sittler, 1950; Darryl Stingley, 1951;
Rick Pitino, 1952; Dennis Johnson, 1954; Billy Sims, 1955;
Peter Stastny, 1956; Ryne Sandberg, 1959; Toni Kukoc, 1968;
Lance Armstrong, 1971; Ronaldo, 1976; Dashon Goldson, 1984;
Serge Ibaka, 1989

On This Day: In 1968, Cardinals pitcher Ray Washburn no-hit
the Giants at Candlestick Park, 2-0. The pitching gem came the day
after Gaylord Perry of the Giants had no-hit St. Louis, 1-0. These
games marked the only time that no-hitters have been thrown on
successive days in the same ballpark.

Trivia Answer: The Polo Grounds

SEPTEMBER

19

Today's Trivia: On September 19, 2011, who passed Trevor Hoffman to become Major League Baseball's all-time leader in saves when he recorded #602?

Birthdays: Charlie Conerly, 1921; Willie Pep, 1922; Duke Snider, 1926; Bob Turley, 1930; Joe Morgan, 1943; Sidney Wicks, 1949; Dan Hampton, 1957; Randy Myers, 1962; Jim Abbott, 1967; Dan Bylsma, 1970; Brett Keisel, 1978; Gio Gonzalez, 1985; Tyreke Evans, 1989; C.J. McCollum, 1991

On This Day: In 1925, Bill Tilden became the first tennis player in the modern era to win six straight U.S. Opens (then known as National Championships). Four years later, Tilden would win number seven.

Trivia Answer: Mariano Rivera

SEPTEMBER

20

Today's Trivia: On September 20, 1998, Cal Ripken, Jr. removed himself from the Orioles lineup, ending his record of consecutive games played at 2,632. What fellow Oriole would have a streak of 1,152 that lasted from 2000 to 2007?

Birthdays: Harry Litwack, 1907; Red Auerbach, 1917; Jim Taylor, 1935;   Tom Tresh, 1938; Tommy Nobis, 1943; Guy Lafleur, 1951; Jason Bay, 1978; Dante Hall, 1978; Ian Desmond, 1985; Coby Fleener, 1988; John Tavares, 1990; Carlos Hyde, 1991

On This Day: In 1973, Billie Jean King defeated Bobby Riggs in a "Battle of the Sexes" tennis match. An estimated 90 million people worldwide tuned in for the $100,000 winner-take-all competition at Houston's Astrodome. King, 26 years younger than Riggs, cruised to victory, 6-4, 6-3, 6-3.

Trivia Answer: Miguel Tejada

SEPTEMBER

Today's Trivia: On September 21, 1970, what team defeated the New York Jets in the first-ever *Monday Night Football* broadcast?

Birthdays: Howie Morenz, 1902; Doug Moe, 1938; Sam McDowell, 1942; Artis Gilmore, 1949; Bob Huggins, 1953; Sidney Moncrief, 1957; Rick Mahorn, 1958; Cecil Fielder, 1963; Jon Kitna, 1972; Scott Spiezio, 1972; Kevin Carter, 1973; Greg Jennings, 1983; Dwayne Bowe, 1984; Doug Baldwin, 1988; Carlos Martinez, 1991

On This Day: In 1955, Rocky Marciano won the last title bout of his undefeated career with a ninth round knockout of Archie Moore. Exactly 30 years later, Larry Holmes' bid to join Marciano as the only heavyweight to win 49 fights without a loss ended with a close decision in favor of opponent Michael Spinks.

Trivia Answer: Cleveland Browns

SEPTEMBER

Today's Trivia: On September 22, 1991, the NFL's all-time winningest head coach won his 300th game. Who is he?

Birthdays: Bob Lemon, 1920; Tommy Lasorda, 1927; Ingemar Johansson, 1932; Lute Olson, 1934; David Stern, 1942; Larry Dierker, 1946; Harold Carmichael, 1949; Jeffrey Leonard, 1955; Vince Coleman, 1961; Mike Richter, 1966; Mike Matheny, 1970; Swin Cash, 1979; Alexei Ramirez, 1981; Denard Robinson, 1990; Carlos Correa, 1994

On This Day: In 1927, Gene Tunney defeated Jack Dempsey in the controversial "Long Count Fight" to retain his heavyweight title. In the seventh round, Tunney hit the ground. Dempsey was slow to move to a neutral corner, thus delaying the count on Tunney, who was able to get up before the referee reached "10". He would wind up winning after 10 rounds in a unanimous decision.

Trivia Answer: Don Shula

SEPTEMBER 23

Today's Trivia: On September 23, 1908, an all-time blunder ultimately cost the Giants the pennant. What player's failure to touch second base resulted in his teammate's winning run being disallowed?

Birthdays: Peter Thompson, 1929; Marty Schottenheimer, 1943; Al Richardson, 1957; Marvin Lewis, 1958; Larry Mize, 1958; John Harbaugh, 1962; Pete Harnisch, 1966; Tony Mandarich, 1966; Jeff Cirillo, 1969; Ricky Davis, 1979; Matt Kemp, 1984; Joba Chamberlain, 1985; Chris Johnson, 1985; Brandon Jennings, 1989

On This Day: In 1957, Hank Aaron's 11th inning home run powered the Braves past the Cardinals, 4-2, clinching the National League pennant, their first in Milwaukee. The Braves would win the World Series over the Yankees.

Trivia Answer: Fred Merkle (Rather than going from first to second on a teammate's hit, Merkle ran back to the dugout as he watched the "winning" run score from third. He was then thrown out. The sequence is infamously known as Merkle's Boner.)

SEPTEMBER 24

Today's Trivia: On September 24, 1994, Kordell Stewart's Hail Mary pass to Michael Westbrook gave what school a stunning 27-26 last-second win over Michigan?

Birthdays: Jim McKay, 1921; John Mackey, 1941; "Mean" Joe Greene, 1946; Terry Metcalf, 1951; Hubie Brooks, 1956; Rafael Palmeiro, 1964; Bernard Gilkey, 1966; Kevin Millar, 1971; Eddie George, 1973; Kabeer Gbaja-Biamila, 1977; Drew Gooden, 1981; Morgan & Paul Hamm, 1982; Randy Foye, 1983; Travis Ishikawa, 1983; Vontaze Burfict, 1990

On This Day: In 1988, USA's Jackie Joyner-Kersee set a heptathlon women's record of 7,291 points to win the gold at the Seoul Summer Games. That very same day, Canada's Ben Johnson won gold in the 100-meter dash. Johnson's glory, however, was short-lived. Three days later, he tested positive for steroids and was stripped of his medal.

Trivia Answer: Colorado

SEPTEMBER

25

Today's Trivia: On September 25, 2006, the Saints played their first game in New Orleans since Hurricane Katrina devastated the city the previous year. Whose block of a punt that was returned for a score marked one of the most dramatic moments in team history?

Birthdays: Red Smith, 1905; Phil Rizzuto, 1917; Johnny Sain, 1917; Hubie Brown, 1933; Bob McAdoo, 1951; Scottie Pippen, 1965; David Weathers, 1969; Tony Womack, 1969; John Lynch, 1971; Matt Hasselbeck, 1975; Chauncey Billups, 1976; Rocco Baldelli, 1981; Aldon Smith, 1989; Brandin Cooks, 1993

On This Day: In 2014, Derek Jeter said goodbye to Yankee Stadium in legendary fashion. In his final at bat in his final home game, Jeter was the hero when he singled in the winning run to give the Yankees a 6-5 victory over the Orioles.

Trivia Answer: Steve Gleason (Curtis Deloatch recovered the ball for a TD.)

SEPTEMBER

26

Today's Trivia: On September 26, 1973, what basketball legend signed on as a player-coach with the San Diego Conquistadors?

Birthdays: Bobby Shantz, 1925; Dave Casper, 1951; Rich Gedman, 1959; Dave Martinez, 1964; Craig Heyward, 1966; T.J. Houshmandzadeh, 1977; Daniel & Henrik Sedin, 1980; Serena Williams, 1981; D'Qwell Jackson, 1983; Chris Archer, 1988; Michael Kidd-Gilchrist, 1993

On This Day: In 1999, the Americans defeated the Europeans in the largest final day come-from-behind victory in Ryder Cup history. Justin Leonard became the hero with a 45-foot birdie putt on the 17th hole as his team won the "Battle of Brookline" by a margin of 14 ½ to 13 ½.

Trivia Answer: Wilt Chamberlain (He would wind up coaching the team, not playing.)

SEPTEMBER

27

Today's Trivia: On September 27, 2000, what U.S. Greco-Roman wrestler stunned Russia's Aleksandr Karelin, who was undefeated in over a decade of international competition, to win gold at the Sydney Olympics?

Birthdays: Johnny Pesky, 1919; Dick Schaap, 1934; Kathy Whitworth, 1939; Mike Schmidt, 1949; Steve Kerr, 1965; Rob Moore, 1968; Alonzo Spellman, 1971; Vicente Padilla, 1977; Jon Garland, 1979

On This Day: In 1930, Bobby Jones won the U.S. Amateur, giving him a sweep of golf's major tournaments and the sport's first-ever "Grand Slam." Jones already had won the British Amateur, the British Open and the U.S. Open that year.

Trivia Answer: Rulon Gardner

SEPTEMBER

28

Today's Trivia: On September 28, 1951, what Rams quarterback set a record that still stands when he threw for 554 yards in a single game?

Birthdays: Ellsworth Vines, 1911; Alice Marble, 1913; Tom Harmon, 1919; Charley Taylor, 1941; Mel Gray, 1948; Steve Largent, 1954; Rob Manfred, 1958; Todd Worrell, 1959; Irving Fryar, 1962; Grant Fuhr, 1962; Johnny Dawkins, 1963; Jake Reed, 1967; Brian Rafalski, 1973; Bonzi Wells, 1976; Jose Calderon, 1981; Emeka Okafor, 1982; Anderson Varejao, 1982; Ryan Zimmerman, 1984

On This Day: In 1941, Ted Williams had four hits in five at bats in the first game of a doubleheader in Philadelphia to bring his average to .404. He went 2-for-3 in game two to finish the season with a .406 batting average. Nineteen years later to the day, Teddy Ballgame homered in the final at bat of his Major League career.

Trivia Answer: Norm Van Brocklin

SEPTEMBER

Today's Trivia: On September 29, 2002, what Raider surpassed Walter Payton's NFL career record of 21,264 yards from scrimmage?

Birthdays: Bum Phillips, 1923; Chuck Cooper, 1926; Mike McCormick, 1938; Bryant Gumbel, 1948; Steve Busby, 1949; Warren Cromartie, 1953; Sebastian Coe, 1956; Rob Deer, 1960; John Paxson, 1960; Hersey Hawkins, 1966; Ken Norton Jr., 1966; Ray Buchanan, 1971; Heath Bell, 1977; Jake Westbrook, 1977; Calvin Johnson, 1985; Kevin Durant, 1988

On This Day: In 1954, Willie Mays made one of the most iconic catches in MLB history with a running, over-the-shoulder grab of a Vic Wertz 450-foot drive to center field. The play came in Game 1 of the World Series, which the New York Giants would go on to sweep over the Cleveland Indians.

Trivia Answer: Jerry Rice

SEPTEMBER

Today's Trivia: On September 30, 1962, what team finished off a disastrous inaugural MLB season by losing their 120th game of the season?

Birthdays: Robin Roberts, 1926; Johnny Podres, 1932; Dave Magadan, 1962; Jamal Anderson, 1972; Jose Lima, 1972; Carlos Guillen, 1975; Justin Smith, 1979; Martina Hingis, 1980; Dominique Moceanu, 1981; Adam "Pac-Man" Jones, 1983; Kenley Jansen, 1987

On This Day: In 1927, Babe Ruth became the first player to hit 60 home runs in one season. The drive off pitcher Tom Zachary broke a 2-2 tie and propelled the Yankees to a 4-2 win over Washington in the next-to-last game of the season.

Trivia Answer: New York Mets

OCTOBER

Today's Trivia: On October 1, 1975, Muhammad
Ali retained his world heavyweight title by defeating Joe
Frazier in the Philippines in a fight that's best known by what
nickname?

Birthdays: Rod Carew, 1945; Grete Waitz, 1953;
Jeff Reardon, 1955; Mark McGwire, 1963; Roberto Kelly, 1964;
Cliff Ronning, 1965; Rudi Johnson, 1979; Matt Cain, 1984;
Xander Bogaerts, 1992

On This Day: In 1961, the Yankees' Roger Maris broke the
record many thought would never be broken when he hit his 61st
home run in the final game of the season. Maris' blast off Tracy
Stallard of the Red Sox bettered Babe Ruth's mark of 60, which
had stood for 34 years.

Trivia Answer: The Thrilla in Manila

OCTOBER

Today's Trivia: On October 2, 1978, whose
three-run home run ultimately clinched the division for
the Yankees in their one-game playoff against the Red Sox at
Fenway Park?

Birthdays: Maury Wills, 1932; Dick Barnett, 1936;
Chuck Pagano, 1960; Mark Rypien, 1962; Thomas Muster, 1967;
Eddie Guardado, 1970; Tyson Chandler, 1982

On This Day: In 1968, Bob Gibson got his St. Louis Cardinals
off to a good start in the first game of the World Series, striking out
17 Detroit batters in a 4-0 win. Five years earlier to the day, Sandy
Koufax fanned 15 in a Dodgers Game 1 Series victory over the
Yankees.

Trivia Answer: Bucky Dent

OCTOBER

Today's Trivia: On October 3, 2012, who finished the regular season with a .330 batting average, 44 home runs and 139 RBIs to become baseball's first Triple Crown winner since 1967?

Birthdays: Jean Ratelle, 1940; Dave Winfield, 1951; Bruce Arians, 1952; Dennis Eckersley, 1954; Fred Couples, 1959; Darrin Fletcher, 1966; Wil Cordero, 1971; Anquan Boldin, 1980

On This Day: In 1951, Bobby Thomson's ninth inning, three-run blast off Ralph Branca gave the New York Giants a 5-4 win over the Brooklyn Dodgers in the third game of their playoff - and the pennant. "The Shot Heard 'Round the World" ended a comeback that had started with the Giants trailing the Dodgers by 13.5 games in mid-August.

Trivia Answer: Miguel Cabrera

OCTOBER

Today's Trivia: On October 4, 2014, what team defeated the Washington Nationals in Game 2 of the NLDS in the longest postseason contest in MLB history?

Birthdays: Sam Huff, 1934; Tony La Russa, 1944; A.C. Green, 1963; Bobby Bonilla, 1964; Mark McLemore, 1964; Kurt Thomas, 1972; Kyle Lohse, 1978; Justin Williams, 1981; Jered Weaver, 1982; Kurt Suzuki, 1983; Derrick Rose, 1988

On This Day: In 1955, the Dodgers won their first and only World Series in Brooklyn when they defeated the Yankees in seven games. After victories in Games 3 and 7, Brooklyn pitcher Johnny Podres was named the first-ever World Series MVP.

Trivia Answer: San Francisco Giants, 2-1, in 18 innings

OCTOBER

5

Today's Trivia: On October 5, 2001, Barry Bonds passed Mark McGwire with his 71st home run of the season. The man with the most career wins of any Asian-born pitcher gave it up. Who?

Birthdays: Barry Switzer, 1937; Michael Andretti, 1962; Laura Davies, 1963; Mario Lemieux, 1965; Patrick Roy, 1965; Dennis Byrd, 1966; Rex Chapman, 1967; Grant Hill, 1972; Trent Cole, 1982; Alexi Ogando, 1983; Travis Kelce, 1989

On This Day: In 1953, the New York Yankees clinched their fifth consecutive World Series title, which remains a record to this day. Billy Martin singled in the winning run in the bottom of the ninth to defeat the Dodgers in six games.

Trivia Answer: Chan Ho Park, then with the Dodgers

OCTOBER

6

Today's Trivia: On October 6, 2010, who threw a no-hitter against the Cincinnati Reds in the first postseason start of his career?

Birthdays: Helen Wills Moody, 1905; Tony Dungy, 1955; Dennis "Oil Can" Boyd, 1959; Albert Lewis, 1960; Ruben Sierra, 1965; Darren Oliver, 1970; J.J. Stokes, 1972; Rebecca Lobo, 1973; Freddy Garcia, 1976; Richard Seymour, 1979; Joel Hanrahan, 1981

On This Day: In 1926, Babe Ruth became the first player to hit three home runs in a World Series game. His efforts led the Yankees to a 10-5 win against the Cardinals in Game 4. New York, however, would lose the Series in seven. Ruth would duplicate his feat of three homers in the 1928 Fall Classic – also in Game 4, and also against the Cards. This time, the Yanks swept St. Louis.

Trivia Answer: Roy Halladay, for the Phillies

OCTOBER

7

Today's Trivia: On October 7, 2012, what quarterback broke Johnny Unitas' long-standing record when he threw a touchdown pass in a 48th consecutive game?

Birthdays: Chuck Klein, 1904; Willie Naulls, 1934; Dick Jauron, 1950; Blair Thomas, 1967; Johnnie Morton, 1971; Priest Holmes, 1973; Charles Woodson, 1976; Evan Longoria, 1985; Jairus Byrd, 1986; Mookie Betts, 1992

On This Day: In 1984, Walter Payton became the NFL's all-time leading rusher with 154 yards in a Bears 20-7 win over New Orleans. Payton's performance gave him 12,400 career rushing yards, breaking the record held by Jim Brown. (Emmitt Smith currently owns the career rushing record with 18,355 yards.)

Trivia Answer: Drew Brees

OCTOBER

8

Today's Trivia: On October 8, 1961, what Yankee and eventual World Series MVP set a Fall Classic record when he surpassed 30 straight scoreless innings with five innings of shutout ball against the Reds in Game 4?

Birthdays: Billy Conn, 1917; Fred Stolle, 1938; Bill Elliott, 1955; Tony Eason, 1959; Mike Morgan, 1959; Matt Biondi, 1965; Donnie Abraham, 1973; Rashaan Salaam, 1974

On This Day: In 1956, Yankees pitcher Don Larsen hurled the only perfect game in World Series history, posting a 2-0 Game 5 win over the Brooklyn Dodgers. Larsen threw just 97 pitches and struck out seven, including Dale Mitchell for the climactic last out. The feat was even more improbable considering Larsen couldn't get out of the second inning of his first start against Brooklyn in Game 2.

Trivia Answer: Whitey Ford

OCTOBER

9

Today's Trivia: On October 9, 1989, the first black NFL head coach of the modern era won his first game when the Raiders defeated the Jets. Who is he?

Birthdays: Rube Marquard, 1889; Walter O'Malley, 1903; Joe Pepitone, 1940; Freddie Patek, 1944; Mike Singletary, 1958; Kenny Anderson, 1970; Annika Sorenstam, 1970; Brian Roberts, 1977; Darius Miles, 1981; Derek Holland, 1986; Starling Marte, 1988

On This Day: In 1916, Boston's Babe Ruth showcased his talents in the World Series - as a pitcher. Ruth allowed a first-inning home run and then shut out Brooklyn over the next 13 innings for a 2-1 victory. The Sox would win the Series in five games. Fifty years later to the day, the Baltimore Orioles won their first World Series by sweeping the Dodgers.

Trivia Answer: Art Shell

OCTOBER

10

Today's Trivia: On October 10, 2011, what Ranger became the first player to hit a walk-off grand slam in a postseason game when he took down the Tigers?

Birthdays: Gene Tenace, 1946; Gus Williams, 1953; Derrick McKey, 1966; Brett Favre, 1969; Dale Earnhardt Jr., 1974; Chris Pronger, 1974; Placido Polanco, 1975; Pat Burrell, 1976; Noah Lowry, 1980; Paul Posluszny, 1984; Troy Tulowitzki, 1984; Andrew McCutchen, 1986; Ryan Mathews, 1987; Jeurys Familia, 1989; Shelby Miller, 1990; Geno Smith, 1990; Michael Carter-Williams, 1991

On This Day: In 1968, Mickey Lolich won for the third time in the World Series as his Detroit Tigers defeated the St. Louis Cardinals, 4-1, in Game 7. Lolich, the MVP, allowed just five runs in his three complete games, as the Tigers rallied after losing three of the first four contests.

Trivia Answer: Nelson Cruz

OCTOBER

11

Today's Trivia: On October 11, 1948, what team won their last World Series to date with a Game 6 triumph over the Braves?

Birthdays: Maria Bueno, 1939; Norm Nixon, 1955; Steve Young, 1961; Chris Spielman, 1965; Orlando "El Duque" Hernandez, 1965; Gregg Olson, 1966; Dmitri Young, 1973; Jason Arnott, 1974; Desmond Mason, 1977; Ty Wigginton, 1977; Terrell Suggs, 1982; Mike Conley, Jr., 1987; Michelle Wie, 1989

On This Day: In 1991, Chip Beck tied pro golf's all-time low score for 18 holes, shooting a 13-under-par 59 at the Las Vegas Invitational. Five pars and 13 birdies (a PGA Tour record) enabled Beck to match Al Geiberger's 59 in the 1977 Memphis Classic.

Trivia Answer: Cleveland Indians

OCTOBER

12

Today's Trivia: On October 12, 1979, Chris Ford of the Celtics did something that had never been done before in an NBA game with a single shot. What was it?

Birthdays: Joe Cronin, 1906; Tony Kubek, 1935; Sid Fernandez, 1962; Luis Polonia, 1964; Chris Chandler, 1965; Leon Lett, 1968; Jose Valentin, 1969; Charlie Ward, 1970; Marion Jones, 1975; Bode Miller, 1977; Ryan Clark, 1979; Adrian Wilson, 1979

On This Day: In 1986, Dave Henderson's two-run home run with Boston one strike away from elimination gave the Red Sox a 6-5 lead in Game 5 of the ALCS. After the Angels tied the game, Henderson's sacrifice fly in the 11th inning gave the Sox a 7-6 win. Boston would win the pennant in seven games.

Trivia Answer: Ford hit the first three-pointer in NBA history.

OCTOBER 13

Today's Trivia: On October 13, 1967, the Oakland Oaks defeated the Anaheim Amigos in the inaugural game of what league?

Birthdays: Nathaniel "Sweetwater" Clifton, 1922; Eddie Mathews, 1931; Jerry Jones, 1942; Rich Kotite, 1942; Pat Day, 1953; Reggie Theus, 1957; Doc Rivers, 1961; Derek Harper, 1961; Jerry Rice, 1962; Scott Cooper, 1967; Trevor Hoffman, 1967; Javier Sotomayor, 1967; Nancy Kerrigan, 1969; Summer Sanders, 1972; Brian Dawkins, 1973; Paul Pierce, 1977; Jermaine O'Neal, 1978; Ian Thorpe, 1982; Brian Hoyer, 1985

On This Day: In 1960, Bill Mazeroski's legendary leadoff homer in the bottom of the ninth inning of Game 7 of the World Series gave the Pirates a 10-9 win over the Yankees. It was Pittsburgh's first World Series championship in 35 years.

Trivia Answer: American Basketball Association

OCTOBER 14

Today's Trivia: On October 14, 1976, the Yankees clinched their 30th pennant when whose home run gave them a 7-6 win over the Royals?

Birthdays: John Wooden, 1910; Jerry Glanville, 1941; Al Oliver, 1946; Charlie Joiner, 1947; Sheila Young, 1950; Beth Daniel, 1956; Keith Byars, 1963; Joe Girardi, 1964; P.J. Brown, 1969; Jim Jackson, 1970; Frank Wycheck, 1971; Floyd Landis, 1975; Javon Walker, 1978; Brandon Weeden, 1983; LaRon Landry, 1984; Justin Forsett, 1985; Wesley Matthews, 1986; Jared Goff, 1994

On This Day: In 2003, Steve Bartman went from anonymity to sports infamy after a single foul ball. In Game 6 of the NLCS, the Cubs, up 3-0 on the Marlins, were just five outs from the World Series when Chicago's Moises Alou was positioned to catch a foul ball for an out – until Bartman interfered. The Cubs would surrender eight runs in the inning, and lose the game. They lost Game 7 the following day.

Trivia Answer: Chris Chambliss

OCTOBER

15

Today's Trivia: On October 15, 2005, USC kept its undefeated season going by defeating Notre Dame, 34-31. In a controversial ending, Reggie Bush appeared to illegally push what quarterback across the goal line for the winning score?

Birthdays: John L. Sullivan, 1858; Mel Harder, 1909; Jim Palmer, 1945; Joe Klecko, 1953; Arron Afflalo, 1985; Blaine Gabbert, 1989

On This Day: In 1988, Kirk Gibson hit a dramatic walk-off homer to give the Dodgers Game 1 of the World Series over the A's. An injured Gibson hobbled to the plate in the bottom of the ninth to pinch-hit and face Dennis Eckersley. His two-run shot gave L.A. a 5-4 win. The Dodgers would take the Series in five.

Trivia Answer: Matt Leinart

OCTOBER

16

Today's Trivia: On October 16, 1968, a black gloved-salute during the medal ceremony from what two U.S. runners became one of the most memorable images in Olympic history?

Birthdays: Dave DeBusschere, 1940; Tim McCarver, 1941; Brian Harper, 1959; Kevin McReynolds, 1959; Chris Doleman, 1961; Manute Bol, 1962; Kordell Stewart, 1972; Paul Kariya, 1974; Jermaine Lewis, 1974; Sue Bird, 1980; Jonathan Schoop, 1991; Bryce Harper, 1992

On This Day: In 1969, the New York Mets completed their upset of Baltimore, downing the Orioles, 5-3, and becoming World Champions for the first time. After losing Game 1, the Miracle Mets won the next four to dispose of the favored Birds.

Trivia Answer: Tommie Smith and John Carlos

OCTOBER

17

Today's Trivia: On October 17, 1974, what team beat the Dodgers in five games to become the only team other than the Yankees to win three consecutive Fall Classics?

Birthdays: Red Rolfe, 1908; Jim Gilliam, 1928; Steve "Snapper" Jones, 1942; Bob Seagren, 1946; Danny Ferry, 1966; Ernie Els, 1969; John Rocker, 1974; Holly Holm, 1981; Carlos Gonzalez, 1985

On This Day: In 1989, the Giants and A's were preparing to play Game 3 of the World Series at Candlestick Park when a massive earthquake struck the Bay Area, causing a 10-day disruption to the Fall Classic. When play resumed, Oakland went on to win in a sweep over San Francisco.

Trivia Answer: Oakland A's

OCTOBER

18

Today's Trivia: On October 18, 1977, Reggie Jackson hit three home runs in a Yankees World Series-clinching win over the Dodgers. What two 2000s players have since matched Mr. October's single-game Fall Classic feat?

Birthdays: Nat Holman, 1896; Keith Jackson, 1928; Andy Carey, 1931; Forrest Gregg, 1933; Boyd Dowler, 1937; Mike Ditka, 1939; Willie Horton, 1942; Frank Beamer, 1946; George Hendrick, 1949; Martina Navratilova, 1956; Thomas "Hitman" Hearns, 1958; Lindsey Vonn, 1984; Yoenis Cespedes, 1985; Brittney Griner, 1990

On This Day: In 1924, Red Grange put on one of the greatest shows in the history of college football when his Illinois squad defeated Michigan, 39-14. After running back the opening kick 95 yards for a touchdown, he scored on runs of 67, 56 and 44 yards – all in the first quarter. He added two TDs later in the game, accounting for 402 yards in all.

Trivia Answer: Albert Pujols and Pablo Sandoval

OCTOBER

Today's Trivia: On October 19, 2014, Peyton Manning threw his 509th career TD pass in a Broncos win over the 49ers when he connected with Demaryius Thomas. In doing so, Manning broke the record of what Hall of Famer?

Birthdays: Mordecai Brown, 1876; Lynn Dickey, 1949; Lionel Hollins, 1953; Evander Holyfield, 1962; Webster Slaughter, 1964; Brad Daugherty, 1965; Keith Foulke, 1972; Michael Young, 1976; Jose Bautista, 1980; J.A. Happ, 1982; Daniel Descalso, 1986

On This Day: In 1999, the Braves advanced to their fifth World Series of the decade when Mets pitcher Kenny Rogers walked Andruw Jones to force in the winning run for a 10-9 Atlanta win in Game 6. Exactly seven years later, the Mets experienced more heartbreak in the NLCS when the visiting Cardinals took Game 7 from them, 3-1, in the last playoff game ever played at Shea Stadium.

Trivia Answer: Brett Favre (Manning finished his career with 539 TD passes.)

OCTOBER

Today's Trivia: On October 20, 1968, whose revolutionary leaping technique earned him Olympic gold in the high jump at the Mexico City Games?

Birthdays: Mickey Mantle, 1931; Roosevelt Brown, 1932; Juan Marichal, 1937; Keith Hernandez, 1953; Lee Roy Selmon, 1954; Aaron Pryor, 1955; Dave Krieg, 1958; Juan Gonzalez, 1969; Herman Moore, 1969; Eddie Jones, 1971; Jamie Collins, 1989; Jeremy Hill, 1992; Rodney Hood, 1992

On This Day: In 2004, the Red Sox won the ALCS with a 10-3 victory over the Yankees, coming back in historic fashion from a 3-0 deficit in the best of seven series. Boston would go on to sweep the World Series against St. Louis seven days later, winning their first title in, as one Sox fan's sign said, "86 years, 1,033 months, 31,458 days - but who's counting?"

Trivia Answer: Dick Fosbury (the "Fosbury Flop")

OCTOBER

21

Today's Trivia: On October 21, 2015, the Mets swept the Cubs to advance to the World Series. In doing so, what NLCS MVP set a new postseason record when he homered for the sixth consecutive game?

Birthdays: Whitey Ford, 1928; Vern Mikkelsen, 1928; Lou Lamoriello, 1942; Bill Russell, 1948; Mike Keenan, 1949; George Bell, 1959; Mo Lewis, 1969; Joey Harrington, 1978; Khalil Greene, 1979; Willis McGahee, 1981; Zack Greinke, 1983; Ricky Rubio, 1990

On This Day: In 1980, the third time was the charm for the Philadelphia Phillies. After losing the World Series in 1915 and 1950, the Phils won their first championship, clinching it in six games with a 4-1 victory over the Kansas City Royals. Game 6 remains the most-watched in World Series history.

Trivia Answer: Daniel Murphy

OCTOBER

22

Today's Trivia: On October 22, 2000, Roger Clemens infamously threw the barrel of what Met's shattered bat back in his direction during Game 2 of the Yankees-Mets World Series?

Birthdays: Jimmie Foxx, 1907; Pete Pihos, 1923; Slater Martin, 1925; Wilbur Wood, 1941; Butch Goring, 1949; Jan Stephenson, 1951; Leonard Marshall, 1961; Brian Boitano, 1963; Drazen Petrovic, 1964; Ichiro Suzuki, 1973; Miroslav Satan, 1974; Brad Stevens, 1976; Robinson Cano, 1982; Heath Miller, 1982; Deontay Wilder, 1985; Muhammad Wilkerson, 1989

On This Day: In 1972 and '75, the Cincinnati Reds lost and won, respectively, Game 7 of the World Series. In '72 they fell to the A's, 3-2. In '75, the Reds beat the Red Sox, 4-3, on a ninth-inning Joe Morgan single.

Trivia Answer: Mike Piazza

OCTOBER

23

Today's Trivia: On October 23, 2000, what team came back from a 30-7 fourth quarter deficit to stun the Miami Dolphins in a "Monday Night Miracle"?

Birthdays: Vern Stephens, 1920; John Heisman, 1869; Gertrude Ederle, 1905; Frank "Bruiser" Kinard, 1914; Jim Bunning, 1931; Chi Chi Rodriguez, 1935; Pelé, 1940; Doug Flutie, 1962; Mike Tomczak, 1962; Al Leiter, 1965; Kazuo Matsui, 1975; Keith Van Horn, 1975; John Lackey, 1978

On This Day: In 1993, Toronto's Joe Carter hit the second walk-off homer ever to end a World Series. His three-run shot off Philadelphia's Mitch Williams gave Toronto an 8-6, Game 6 victory for their second consecutive World Series title.

Trivia Answer: New York Jets

OCTOBER

24

Today's Trivia: On October 24, 1992, the Blue Jays became the first World Series champions from outside the U.S. when they defeated what team in six games?

Birthdays: Y.A. Tittle, 1926; Ron Gardenhire, 1957; Rafael Belliard, 1961; Jay Novacek, 1962; Arthur Rhodes, 1969; Pat Williams, 1972; Corey Dillon, 1974; Rafael Furcal, 1977; Eric Hosmer, 1989; Nikola Vucevic, 1990; Jalen Ramsey, 1994

On This Day: In 1959, Wilt Chamberlain made his professional debut. The rookie center scored 43 points and pulled down 28 rebounds as his Philadelphia Warriors beat the New York Knicks, 118-109.

Trivia Answer: Atlanta Braves

OCTOBER 25

Today's Trivia: On October 25, 1964, what Viking provided an NFL blooper-reel fixture when he recovered a fumble and ran 66 yards the wrong way into his own end zone for a safety?

Birthdays: Jack Kent Cooke, 1912; Lee MacPhail, 1917; Bobby Thomson, 1923; Bob Knight, 1940; Dave Cowens, 1948; Dan Issel, 1948; Dan Gable, 1948; Pat Swilling, 1964; Pedro Martinez, 1971; Chandler Parsons, 1988

On This Day: In 1986, a two-out error by Bill Buckner in the bottom of the tenth inning allowed the Mets to get by Boston, 6-5, and force a seventh game in the World Series. The Mets bunched together three hits, a wild pitch and Buckner's error to erase a two-run deficit. The Sox, of course, lost Game 7.

Trivia Answer: Jim Marshall

OCTOBER 26

Today's Trivia: On October 26, 2002, the Angels stunned the Giants to win Game 6 of the World Series after trailing 5-0. What unofficial mascot came to national attention as Anaheim came all the way back to win the title the following night?

Birthdays: Primo Carnera, 1906; Sid Gillman, 1911; Joe Fulks, 1921; Toby Harrah, 1948; Mike Hargrove, 1949; Steve Rogers, 1949; Tom Condon, 1952; Bob Golic, 1957; Jessie Armstead, 1970; Miikka Kiprusoff, 1976; Antonio Pierce, 1978; Francisco Liriano, 1983; Andrea Bargnani, 1985; Monta Ellis, 1985

On This Day: In 1997, the Florida Marlins, in just their fifth MLB season, defeated the Indians, 3-2, in seven games on an Edgar Renteria single in the bottom of the 11th. Exactly eight years later, the White Sox completed a sweep of the Astros to win the team's first championship since 1917.

Trivia Answer: The Rally Monkey

OCTOBER

Today's Trivia: On October 27, 2011, who saved the World Series for the Cardinals with a game-tying triple and a walk-off home run in Game 6 vs. the Rangers?

Birthdays: Ralph Kiner, 1922; Bill George, 1930; Patty Sheehan, 1956; Rick Carlisle, 1959; Bip Roberts, 1963; Mary T. Meagher, 1964; Brad Radke, 1972; Peerless Price, 1976; Jon Niese, 1986; Lou Williams, 1986; Andrew Bynum, 1987; Evan Turner, 1988

On This Day: In 1991, Minnesota's Jack Morris pitched a 10-inning, 1-0 shutout against the Braves in Game 7 of the World Series, giving the Twins their second championship in five years. Five of the Series' contests were decided by a single run.

Trivia Answer: David Freese (The Cards won it in seven.)

OCTOBER

Today's Trivia: On October 28, 1962, what Giants Hall of Famer threw for over 500 yards and tied an NFL record with seven touchdown passes in a win over Washington?

Birthdays: Bowie Kuhn, 1926; Jim Beatty, 1934; Lenny Wilkens, 1937; Caitlyn (Bruce) Jenner, 1949; Lenny Harris, 1964; Steve Atwater, 1966; Juan Guzman, 1966; Terrell Davis, 1972; Calvin Pace, 1980; Nate McLouth, 1981; Jeremy Bonderman, 1982

On This Day: In 1995, MVP Tom Glavine pitched eight innings of one-hit ball to give the Braves a 1-0 victory over the Indians and their third World Series title. In doing so, the Braves became the first team to win a World Series in three cities (Boston, Milwaukee and Atlanta).

Trivia Answer: Y.A. Tittle

OCTOBER

29

Today's Trivia: On October 29, 2014, the Giants defeated the Royals, 3-2, to win the World Series in seven games. After winning Games 1 and 5, who pitched five shutout innings in relief on two days of rest to clinch the MVP award?

Birthdays: Frank Sedgman, 1927; Andy Russell, 1941; Jim Bibby, 1944; Denis Potvin, 1953; J.T. Smith, 1955; Jesse Barfield, 1959; Mike Gartner, 1959; Drew Rosenhaus, 1966; R.A. Dickey, 1974; Travis Henry, 1978; Amanda Beard, 1981; Maurice Clarett, 1983; Andy Dalton, 1987; Evan Fournier, 1992

On This Day: In 1995, Jerry Rice surpassed James Lofton to become the NFL's all-time leading receiver. Rice caught eight passes for 108 yards in a loss to the Saints to boost his total to 14,040. The legacy was far from complete, however, as Rice would end his career with an astounding 22,895 yards receiving.

Trivia Answer: Madison Bumgarner

OCTOBER

30

Today's Trivia: On October 30, 2013, the Boston Red Sox defeated the St. Louis Cardinals to win the World Series in six games. What skipper earned a ring in his first season as Boston's manager?

Birthdays: Charles Atlas, 1892; Bill Terry, 1898; Joe Adcock, 1927; Jim Perry, 1935; Dick Vermeil, 1936; Diego Maradona, 1960; Mark Portugal, 1962; Danny Tartabull, 1962; Keith Brooking, 1975; Marco Scutaro, 1975; Nastia Liukin, 1989; Joe Panik, 1990; Marcus Mariota, 1993

On This Day: In 1974, Muhammad Ali reclaimed the heavyweight title by knocking out previously unbeaten George Foreman in the eighth round in Zaire. The "Rumble in the Jungle" was the first heavyweight championship match held in Africa.

Trivia Answer: John Farrell

OCTOBER

Today's Trivia: On October 31, 1950, who became the first African-American to play in an NBA game?

Birthdays: Cal Hubbard, 1900; Jersey Joe Walcott, 1914; Dave McNally, 1942; Brian Piccolo, 1943; Frank Shorter, 1947; Mickey Rivers, 1948; Nick Saban, 1951; John Lucas, 1953; Mike Gallego, 1960; Bill Fralic, 1962; Fred McGriff, 1963; Matt Nokes, 1963; Antonio Davis, 1968; Lee Woodall, 1969; Steve Trachsel, 1970; Mike Napoli, 1981

On This Day: In 2001, the Yankees shocked the Diamondbacks in Game 4 of the World Series when Tino Martinez hit a two-out, two-run homer in the bottom of the ninth to tie the score at three. That was followed in the tenth by Derek Jeter's solo shot to win it. The game ended after midnight, thus beginning Jeter's "Mr. November" moniker.

Trivia Answer: Earl Lloyd, for the Capitols

NOVEMBER

Today's Trivia: On November 1, 1959, what Canadiens Hall of Famer became the first player in NHL history to wear a full facemask?

Birthdays: Grantland Rice, 1880; Vic Power, 1927; Al Arbour, 1932; Gary Player, 1935; Joe Caldwell, 1941; Ted Hendricks, 1947; Fernando Valenzuela, 1960; Erik Spoelstra, 1970; Steve Hutchinson, 1977; Coco Crisp, 1979; Stephen Vogt, 1984; Bruce Irvin, 1987; Masahiro Tanaka, 1988

On This Day: In 1964, Cleveland's Jim Brown ran for 149 yards against Pittsburgh to become the first NFL player to reach 10,000 career rushing yards. Meanwhile, in the AFL, Houston's George Blanda was taking the high road- through the air - attempting 68 passes (a record that would stand for 30 years) against Buffalo and completing 37 of them.

Trivia Answer: Jacques Plante

NOVEMBER

Today's Trivia: On November 2, 2005, what Lakers All-Star became the youngest player in league history when he made his NBA debut six days after turning 18?

Birthdays: Johnny Vander Meer, 1914; Bill Mosienko, 1921; Ken Rosewall, 1934; Dave Stockton, 1941; Willie McGee, 1958; Mark May, 1959; Bruce Baumgartner, 1960; Orlando Cabrera, 1974; Sidney Ponson, 1976; Martin Grenier, 1980; Roddy White, 1981; Yunel Escobar, 1982; Danny Amendola, 1985; Jimmy Garoppolo, 1991

On This Day: In 1974, the Atlanta Braves traded Hank Aaron to the Milwaukee Brewers for Dave May and Roger Alexander. Aaron spent two seasons with Milwaukee as a designated hitter. Exactly 21 years later, one of Aaron's Braves teammates, Joe Torre, was named the manager of the New York Yankees.

Trivia Answer: Andrew Bynum

NOVEMBER

Today's Trivia: On November 3, 1995, the NBA's first two teams from outside the U.S. each won their debut games. Who are they?

Birthdays: Bronko Nagurski, 1908; Bob Feller, 1918; Roy Emerson, 1936; Ken Holtzman, 1945; Larry Holmes, 1949; Dwight Evans, 1951; Bob Welch, 1956; Phil Simms, 1955; Karch Kiraly, 1960; Armando Benitez, 1972; Darren Sharper, 1975; Pekka Rinne, 1982; Tamba Hali, 1983; LaMarr Woodley, 1984; Tyler Hansbrough, 1985; Colin Kaepernick, 1987; Ty Lawson, 1987; Kyle Seager, 1987

On This Day: In 1990, one of college football's most prolific passing duels took place as Houston defeated Texas Christian, 56-35. Houston's David Klingler threw for 563 yards and seven touchdowns. Meanwhile, TCU's Matt Vogler tossed five TDs to go along with 690 yards through the air.

Trivia Answer: Toronto Raptors and Vancouver (now Memphis) Grizzlies

NOVEMBER

Today's Trivia: On November 4, 2001, the Diamondbacks stunned the Yankees by scoring twice in the bottom of the ninth to win Game 7 of the World Series. Who hit the title-winning single for Arizona?

Birthdays: Dick Groat, 1930; Tito Francona, 1933; Clark Graebner, 1943; Willie Buchanon, 1950; Steve Mariucci, 1955; Eric Karros, 1967; Carlos Baerga, 1968; Orlando Pace, 1975; Vince Wilfork, 1981; Devin Hester, 1982; Dez Bryant, 1988

On This Day: In 2007, the Patriots inched closer to a perfect regular season with a 24-20 defeat of the 7-0 Colts in one of the NFL's most-hyped regular season contests ever. The historic matchup came just hours after Adrian Peterson set a new single-game record with 296 yards rushing in a Vikings win over the Chargers.

Trivia Answer: Luis Gonzalez

NOVEMBER

Today's Trivia: On November 5, 1927, what winner of 11 career majors won the PGA Championship for a fourth consecutive time?

Birthdays: Bill Walton, 1952; Kellen Winslow, 1957; Lloyd Moseby, 1959; Javy Lopez, 1970; Johnny Damon, 1973; Alexei Yashin, 1973; Jerry Stackhouse, 1974; Bubba Watson, 1978; O.J. Mayo, 1987; Odell Beckham, Jr., 1992

On This Day: In 1994, 45-year-old George Foreman knocked out Michael Moorer in the tenth round to become the oldest heavyweight champion in boxing history. Foreman, trailing on all scorecards before the KO, regained the title he lost to Muhammad Ali two decades prior.

Trivia Answer: Walter Hagen

NOVEMBER

Today's Trivia: On November 6, 1974, what
Dodger became the first reliever to win a Cy Young Award?

Birthdays: James Naismith, 1861; Walter Johnson, 1887;
Pat Dye, 1939; John Candelaria, 1953; Mark Haynes, 1958;
Erik Kramer, 1964; Chad Curtis, 1968; Pat Tillman, 1976;
Adam LaRoche, 1979; Lamar Odom, 1979; Ricky Romero, 1984;
Aaron Hernandez, 1989

On This Day: In 1869, Rutgers and Princeton met in New
Brunswick, N.J., in the first college football game. Rutgers won,
6-4, in a contest that featured 25 players on each side and one-point
"touchdowns". Because no throwing or running with the ball was
permitted, the event more closely resembled a soccer match.

Trivia Answer: Mike Marshall

NOVEMBER

Today's Trivia: On November 7, 1963, what
Yankee was named the first black MVP in American
League history?

Birthdays: Dick Stuart, 1932; Al Attles, 1936; Jim Kaat, 1938;
Joe Niekro, 1944; Buck Martinez, 1948; Russ Springer, 1968;
Dave Fleming, 1969; Kris Benson, 1974; Mark Philippoussis, 1976;
Sonny Gray, 1989

On This Day: In 1991, Magic Johnson shocked basketball fans
around the world, announcing his retirement from the NBA because
he was HIV-positive. While the event was marked with sadness,
Magic would return to play in the 1992 All-Star Game, winning
the MVP.

Trivia Answer: Elston Howard (Jackie Robinson was the NL's first.)

NOVEMBER

Today's Trivia: On November 8, 1966, who became the only player to date to be named MVP of both leagues when he was voted the AL MVP as a member of the Orioles?

Birthdays: Frank McGuire, 1916; Bobby Bowden, 1929; Tom "Satch" Sanders, 1938; Angel Cordero Jr., 1942; Ed Kranepool, 1944; Jimmie Giles, 1954; Jeff Blauser, 1965; Jose Offerman, 1968; Qadry Ismail, 1970; Edgardo Alfonzo, 1973; Brevin Knight, 1975; Nick Punto, 1977; Sam Bradford, 1987; Yasmani Grandal, 1988; Giancarlo Stanton, 1989

On This Day: In 1970, Tom Dempsey kicked a record-breaking 63-yard field goal to give the Saints a 19-17 win over the Lions. Dempsey was born without toes on his right foot – his kicking foot. Matt Prater would top Dempsey's mark by hitting a 64-yard field goal in 2013.

Trivia Answer: Frank Robinson (He was the 1961 NL MVP with the Reds.)

NOVEMBER

Today's Trivia: On November 9, 1983, David Stern was named the NBA's new commissioner. What man did he succeed?

Birthdays: Florence Chadwick, 1917; Whitey Herzog, 1931; Bob Gibson, 1935; Tom Weiskopf, 1942; Roy Jefferson, 1943; Teddy Higuera, 1958; David Duval, 1971; Mark Fields, 1972; Jose Rosado, 1974; Adam Dunn, 1979; Owen Daniels, 1982; Joel Zumaya, 1984; Kyle Rudolph, 1989; Greg Bird, 1992

On This Day: In 1989, the Milwaukee Bucks and Seattle SuperSonics battled through five overtime periods in the NBA's longest game of the shot clock era. When it was over, the Bucks were left standing with a 155-154 victory. Dale Ellis scored 53 points for Seattle in the loss.

Trivia Answer: Larry O'Brien

NOVEMBER

10

Today's Trivia: On November 10, 1984, Maryland stunned Miami and all of college football by coming back from 31-0 to win, 42-40. The man who would lead the biggest comeback in NFL history was under center for the Terps that day. Who?

Birthdays: Gene Conley, 1930; Norm Cash, 1934; George Sauer, 1943; Les Miles, 1953; Larry Parrish, 1953; Jack Clark, 1955; Ken Holland, 1955; Mike McCarthy, 1963; Mike Powell, 1963; Kenny Rogers, 1964; Isaac Bruce, 1972; Shawn Green, 1972; Donte' Stallworth, 1980; Kendrick Perkins, 1984; D.J. Augustin, 1987; Zach Ertz, 1990; Teddy Bridgewater, 1992

On This Day: In 1928, fabled football coach Knute Rockne gave his famous "Win one for the Gipper" halftime speech. George Gipp was a Notre Dame All-American who died of pneumonia in 1920. Rockne's underdog Fighting Irish went on to defeat Army, 12-6.

Trivia Answer: Frank Reich (He quarterbacked the Bills in the 1992 postseason.)

NOVEMBER

11

Today's Trivia: On November 11, 1990, who set an NFL single-game record with seven sacks against the Seattle Seahawks?

Birthdays: Pie Traynor, 1899; Bobby Dodd, 1908; Gil Perreault, 1951; Fuzzy Zoeller, 1951; Roberto Hernandez, 1964; Damion Easley, 1969; Jason Grilli, 1976; LaMont Jordan, 1978; Willie Parker, 1980; Victor Cruz, 1986; Mark Sanchez, 1986

On This Day: In 1981, Fernando Valenzuela, the National League Rookie of the Year, made history when he added the league's Cy Young Award to his trophy collection. Exactly 21 years later, Barry Bonds collected his fifth NL MVP, the most in MLB history. He would finish his career with seven.

Trivia Answer: Derrick Thomas, with the Chiefs

NOVEMBER

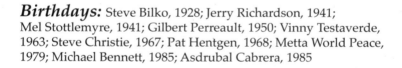

Today's Trivia: On November 12, 1931, Chicago defeated Toronto in the first game played at what historic hockey venue?

Birthdays: Ken Houston, 1944; Al Michaels, 1944; Cliff Harris, 1948; Steve Bartkowski, 1952; Jody Davis, 1956; Nadia Comaneci, 1961; Greg Gagne, 1961; Sammy Sosa, 1968; Tonya Harding, 1970; Corey Maggette, 1979; Lance Briggs, 1980; Jason Day, 1987; Russell Westbrook, 1988; Allen Hurns, 1991; Trey Burke, 1992

On This Day: In 1920, Major League Baseball's owners elected Judge Kenesaw Mountain Landis as the sport's first commissioner. Landis is best remembered for his handling of the Black Sox scandal, in which he banned eight members of the White Sox from baseball for conspiring to fix the 1919 World Series. He would preside over America's national pastime until his death in 1944.

Trivia Answer: Maple Leaf Gardens

NOVEMBER

Today's Trivia: On November 13, 1964, the first person to win the NBA's MVP Award (in 1956) became the first player to score 20,000 career points. Who is he?

Birthdays: Steve Bilko, 1928; Jerry Richardson, 1941; Mel Stottlemyre, 1941; Gilbert Perreault, 1950; Vinny Testaverde, 1963; Steve Christie, 1967; Pat Hentgen, 1968; Metta World Peace, 1979; Michael Bennett, 1985; Asdrubal Cabrera, 1985

On This Day: In 1985, Lynette Woodard became the first woman to play for the Harlem Globetrotters. Woodard, a Basketball Hall of Famer who starred at Kansas and on the 1984 Olympic gold medal team, scored seven points in her debut. She would spend two years with the Globetrotters.

Trivia Answer: Bob Pettit

NOVEMBER

14

Today's Trivia: On November 14, 1943, what Bears Hall of Famer threw for over 400 yards and seven TD passes in a single game, becoming the first NFL player to accomplish either feat?

Birthdays: Jimmy Piersall, 1929; Willie Hernandez, 1954; Jack Sikma, 1955; Aaron Broten, 1960; Curt Schilling, 1966; Dana Stubblefield, 1970; David Wesley, 1970; Lawyer Milloy, 1973; Xavier Nady, 1978; Kyle Orton, 1982; T.Y. Hilton, 1989

On This Day: In 1970, tragedy struck Marshall University when 75 people, including nearly 40 football players and much of the team's coaching staff, were killed in a plane crash near the Tri-State Airport in West Virginia. The team was returning from that day's game, a loss to East Carolina.

Trivia Answer: Sid Luckman

NOVEMBER

15

Today's Trivia: On November 15, 2004, the Eagles defeated the Cowboys on *Monday Night Football*. The game, however, would be overshadowed by a controversial opening skit featuring *Desperate Housewives* star Nicollette Sheridan and what player?

Birthdays: Gus Bell, 1928; Bob Dandridge, 1947; Otis Armstrong, 1950; Mac Wilkens, 1950; Greg Anthony, 1967; Pedro Borbon, 1967; Cory Redding, 1980; Lofa Tatupu, 1982; Trevor Story, 1992; Karl-Anthony Towns, 1995

On This Day: In 1960, Lakers forward Elgin Baylor put on a scoring exhibition at Madison Square Garden. Baylor tallied 71 points in a 123-108 win over the Knicks, breaking his own NBA record of 64 points.

Trivia Answer: Terrell Owens

NOVEMBER

Today's Trivia: On November 16, 1991, #2 Miami took down what rival and #1-ranked team when Gerry Thomas missed a 34-yard field goal attempt with seconds remaining?

Birthdays: Jo Jo White, 1946; Harvey Martin, 1950; Terry Labonte, 1956; Corey Pavin, 1959; Zina Garrison, 1963; Dwight Gooden, 1964; Oksana Baiul, 1977; Osi Umenyiora, 1981; Amar'e Stoudemire, 1982; Marcus McNeill, 1983; Denzel Valentine, 1993

On This Day: In 1957, college football's longest winning streak came to an end. A Dick Lynch touchdown late in the fourth quarter was the only score as Notre Dame upset Oklahoma, 7-0. Up to that point, the Sooners had won 47 straight games.

Trivia Answer: Florida State

NOVEMBER

Today's Trivia: On November 17, 2013, who came in first in the United States Grand Prix to win his eighth consecutive race, the most ever within a single Formula One season?

Birthdays: Joe Mullaney, 1925; Bob Mathias, 1930; Gary Bell, 1936; Jim Boeheim, 1944; Tom Seaver, 1944; Elvin Hayes, 1945; Mitch Williams, 1964; Paul Sorrento, 1965; Jeff Nelson, 1966; Kyle Vanden Bosch, 1978; Reggie Wayne, 1978; Ryan Braun, 1983; Nick Markakis, 1983; Everth Cabrera, 1986

On This Day: In 1968, NBC cut away from the Raiders-Jets football game with a little more than a minute to play to show the movie *Heidi*. The network's offices were deluged with phone calls from angry fans who missed seeing Oakland score two touchdowns in nine seconds to beat New York, 43-32. The contest became forever known as the "Heidi Game."

Trivia Answer: Sebastian Vettel

NOVEMBER

Today's Trivia: On November 18, 1966, what MLB great called it a career at age 30 due to chronic arthritis in his pitching arm?

Birthdays: Phog Allen, 1885; Gene Mauch, 1925; Jack Tatum, 1948; Warren Moon, 1956; Jamie Moyer, 1962; Dante Bichette, 1963; Todd Bowles, 1963; Seth Joyner, 1964; Tom Gordon, 1967; Gary Sheffield, 1968; Sam Cassell, 1969; Raghib "Rocket" Ismail, 1969; David Ortiz, 1975; Jason Williams, 1975; Denny Hamlin, 1980; C.J. Wilson, 1980; Allyson Felix, 1985; Marcell Dareus, 1989

On This Day: In 1985, Redskins quarterback Joe Theismann suffered a gruesome career-ending injury when he was hit by Giants linebacker Lawrence Taylor. Theismann suffered a compound fracture of his right leg in the middle of a *Monday Night Football* game at RFK Stadium. The infamous moment was later used in the opening for the 2009 film *The Blind Side.*

Trivia Answer: Sandy Koufax

NOVEMBER

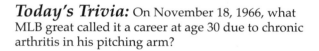

Today's Trivia: On November 19, 1978, a "Miracle at the Meadowlands" occurred when the Giants blew a game vs. the Eagles by calling a run rather than a simple kneel down to seal a victory. After a fumble, what future NFL head coach scooped up the ball and ran in the winning score for Philly?

Birthdays: Roy Campanella, 1921; Ted Turner, 1938; Bob Boone, 1947; Ahmad Rashad, 1949; Richard Todd, 1953; Mike Mularkey, 1961; Gail Devers, 1966; Justin Duchscherer, 1977; Kerri Strug, 1977; Ryan Howard, 1979; Larry Johnson, 1979; DeAngelo Hall, 1983; Alex Mack, 1985; Patrick Kane, 1988; Kenneth Faried, 1989

On This Day: In 2004, the Palace of Auburn Hills was the site of an infamous Pacers-Pistons brawl. The incident involved Indiana's Ron Artest and several others charging into the stands after Artest was hit with a drinking cup by a fan while shamelessly lying on the scorer's table. In all, the NBA suspended nine players for a total of 146 games.

Trivia Answer: Herman Edwards

NOVEMBER

Today's Trivia: On November 20, 1997, who played in his 907th consecutive game, setting a new NBA record?

Birthdays: Kenesaw Mountain Landis, 1866; Don January, 1929; Louie Dampier, 1944; Rick Monday, 1945; Mark Gastineau, 1956; Dwight Stephenson, 1957; Chris Childs, 1967; Dabo Swinney, 1969; Joey Galloway, 1971; J.D. Drew, 1975; Dominique Dawes, 1976; Carlos Boozer, 1981; Greg Holland, 1985

On This Day: In 1982, "The Play" took place at California Memorial Stadium. With Stanford up 20-19 after a field goal with seconds remaining, the California Bears returned the kickoff all the way for a touchdown on a series of laterals. The biggest obstacle to the end zone for the Bears was the Stanford school band, which was out on the field for a premature victory celebration. Cal won, 25-20.

Trivia Answer: A.C. Green

NOVEMBER

Today's Trivia: On November 21, 1996, what head coach, who had won a title with Boston, became the first in NBA history to lose 1,000 games?

Birthdays: Sid Luckman, 1916; Stan Musial, 1920; Jim Ringo, 1931; Earl Monroe, 1944; Cedric Maxwell, 1955; Reggie Lewis, 1965; Troy Aikman, 1966; Ken Griffey Jr., 1969; Michael Strahan, 1971; Hank Blalock, 1980; Alex Tanguay, 1979; Justin Tucker, 1989

On This Day: In 1934, the Yankees purchased outfielder Joe DiMaggio from the San Francisco Seals of the Pacific Coast League for $50,000. Exactly 37 years later, another group of Seals would be reeling. In 1971, the New York Rangers scored eight third-period goals on their way to a 12-1 victory over the California Golden Seals.

Trivia Answer: Bill Fitch, then with the Clippers

NOVEMBER

Today's Trivia: On November 22, 1950, the lowest-scoring game in NBA history took place. What Lakers Hall of Fame big man scored 15 points in his team's 19-18 loss to the Pistons?

Birthdays: Lew Burdette, 1926; Yvan Cournoyer, 1943; Billie Jean King, 1943; Greg Luzinski, 1950; Mark Malone, 1958; Eric Allen, 1965; Boris Becker, 1967; Jay Payton, 1972; Joe Nathan, 1974; Jonny Gomes, 1980; Derrick Johnson, 1982; Yusmeiro Petit, 1984; Oscar Pistorius, 1986; Giovani Bernard, 1991

On This Day: In 1986, Mike Tyson became the youngest man to win a heavyweight title. The 20-year-old boxer captured the WBC crown with a second round TKO of Trevor Berbick. Iron Mike moved to 28-0 in his career.

Trivia Answer: George Mikan

NOVEMBER

Today's Trivia: On November 23, 1989, the Eagles destroyed the Cowboys, 27-0, on Thanksgiving. The hotly-contested affair, in which Dallas coach Jimmy Johnson accused Philly coach Buddy Ryan of trying to hurt certain players, was given what nickname?

Birthdays: Lew Hoad, 1934; Luis Tiant, 1940; Shane Gould, 1956; Andrew Toney, 1957; Robin Roberts, 1960; Daniel Snyder, 1964; Vin Baker, 1971; Saku Koivu, 1974; Jamie Sharper, 1974; Jonathan Papelbon, 1980; Mike Tolbert, 1985

On This Day: In 1984, Doug Flutie's "Hail Mary" pass with six seconds left in the game fell into the hands of receiver Gerard Phelan to give Boston College a dramatic 47-45 win over Miami. Flutie and Miami QB Bernie Kosar combined for 919 passing yards on the day.

Trivia Answer: The Bounty Bowl

NOVEMBER

Today's Trivia: On November 24, 1953, what little-known minor league skipper signed a one-year deal to manage the Brooklyn Dodgers, the team he'd go on to sign 22 more one-year contracts with?

Birthdays: Ducky Medwick, 1911; John Henry Johnson, 1929; Yale Lary, 1930; Oscar Robertson, 1938; Paul Tagliabue, 1940; Dave Bing, 1943; Rudy Tomjanovich, 1948; Randy Velarde, 1962; Ben McDonald, 1967; Keith Primeau, 1971; Ryan Fitzpatrick, 1982; Jimmy Graham, 1986

On This Day: In 1960, Wilt Chamberlain pulled down a record 55 rebounds in a 132-129 loss to the Celtics. The Warriors center topped the mark of 51 set by the man defending him that night, Bill Russell. Wilt went on to collect a record 2,149 boards that season, averaging 27.2 per game, another NBA mark.

Trivia Answer: Walter Alston

NOVEMBER

Today's Trivia: On November 25, 2002, what 28-year-old was hired by the Boston Red Sox as the youngest general manager in MLB history?

Birthdays: Joe DiMaggio, 1914; Lenny Moore, 1933; Joe Gibbs, 1940; Bucky Dent, 1951; Chip Kelly, 1963; Bernie Kosar, 1963; Cris Carter, 1965; Mark Whiten, 1966; Octavio Dotel, 1973; Donovan McNabb, 1976; Nick Swisher, 1980; Dan Carpenter, 1985

On This Day: In 1980, Sugar Ray Leonard regained boxing's welterweight title after Roberto Duran, the defending champion, conceded in the eighth round. Duran, behind in the fight, suddenly told the referee, "No mas, no mas. No more box."

Trivia Answer: Theo Epstein

NOVEMBER

Today's Trivia: On November 26, 2000, what fellow Hall of Famer passed John Havlicek and set a still-standing record when he played in his 1,271st NBA game, the most ever with a single team?

Birthdays: Lefty Gomez, 1908; Jan Stenerud, 1942; Art Shell, 1946; Roger Wehrli, 1947; Harry Carson, 1953; Dale Jarrett, 1956; Harold Reynolds, 1960; Chuck Finley, 1962; Mario Elie, 1963; Jeff Jaeger, 1964; Shawn Kemp, 1969; Matt Garza, 1983; Matt Carpenter, 1985; Avery Bradley, 1990

On This Day: In 1989, the Rams scored 14 points in the final minutes of regulation before beating the Saints, 20-17, in overtime. Flipper Anderson scored the game-tying touchdown and set an NFL record with 336 receiving yards on 15 catches.

Trivia Answer: John Stockton, with the Jazz (His record stands at 1,504 games.)

NOVEMBER

Today's Trivia: On November 27, 1947, what Triple Crown winner did Joe DiMaggio defeat by a controversial single vote to be named the American League's Most Valuable Player?

Birthdays: Chick Hearn, 1916; Dave Giusti, 1939; Mike Scioscia, 1958; Ken O'Brien, 1960; Larry Allen, 1971; Ivan Rodriguez, 1971; Nick Van Exel, 1971; Jon Runyan, 1973; Jimmy Rollins, 1978; Michael Floyd, 1989

On This Day: In 1966, the defense rested. The Redskins outscored the Giants, 72-41, in a game that set the NFL record for total points. In all, 16 touchdowns were scored. Washington kicked the lone field goal with seconds left to break the single-team mark of 70 points set by the Rams in 1950.

Trivia Answer: Ted Williams

NOVEMBER

Today's Trivia: On November 28, 2003, what World Series MVP was dealt for the fifth and final time of his career when the Diamondbacks sent him to Boston?

Birthdays: Paul Warfield, 1942; Dave Righetti, 1958; Johnny Newman, 1963; Walt Weiss, 1963; John Burkett, 1964; Roy Tarpley, 1964; Matt Williams, 1965; Dale Carter, 1969; Robb Nen, 1969; Freddie Mitchell, 1978; Leandro Barbosa, 1982; Andrew Bogut, 1984; Marc-Andre Fleury, 1984; Jarvis Landry, 1992; Chase Elliott, 1995

On This Day: In 1929, Chicago Cardinals running back Ernie Nevers set a record that may never be broken. He scored all 40 of his team's points in a blowout win over the Bears. Not only did Nevers account for six touchdowns...he kicked four extra points.

Trivia Answer: Curt Schilling (He was the co-MVP of the 2001 World Series with Randy Johnson.)

NOVEMBER

Today's Trivia: On November 29, 1997, what legendary Grambling State football coach was on the sidelines for his 588th and final game?

Birthdays: Minnie Minoso, 1925; Vin Scully, 1927; Bill Freehan, 1941; George Thompson, 1947; Steve Timmons, 1958; Howard Johnson, 1960; Mariano Rivera, 1969; Jamal Mashburn, 1972; Russell Wilson, 1988; Sheldon Richardson, 1990; Julius Randle, 1994

On This Day: In 1890, the very first Army-Navy football game was played at West Point, New York. The Midshipmen won, 24-0. Exactly 44 years later, the Detroit Lions began their annual NFL tradition when they played their first Thanksgiving home game, losing to the Chicago Bears, 19-16.

Trivia Answer: Eddie Robinson

NOVEMBER

30

Today's Trivia: On November 30, 1974, what school, behind Anthony Davis' four touchdowns, stunned Notre Dame with 55 unanswered points to come from behind and win, 55-24?

Birthdays: Joe B. Hall, 1928; Bill Walsh, 1931; Paul Westphal, 1950; Bob Tewksbury, 1960; Bo Jackson, 1962; Ray Durham, 1971; Matt Lawton, 1971; Marcellus Wiley, 1974; Shane Victorino, 1980; Rich Harden, 1981

On This Day: In 1987, two-sport star Bo Jackson put on a show for the *Monday Night Football* audience. He rushed for 221 yards and scored three TDs in his fifth NFL game as his Raiders beat Seattle, 37-14. Most memorable was his 91-yard score, untouched, down the sideline, and into the players' tunnel.

Trivia Answer: USC

DECEMBER

1

Today's Trivia: On December 1, 2002, who set a new single-game record for rushing yards by a quarterback with 173, including a 46-yard game-winning TD run in overtime, vs. the Vikings?

Birthdays: Walter Alston, 1911; Marty Marion, 1916; Lee Trevino, 1939; George Foster, 1948; Larry Walker, 1966; Steve Walsh, 1966; Reggie Sanders, 1967; Kirk Rueter, 1970; DeSean Jackson, 1986

On This Day: In 1956, the United States basketball team, led by Bill Russell and K.C. Jones, won the gold medal at the Summer Olympics in Melbourne. The U.S. easily handled the Soviets, 89-55, winning its eighth straight game of the competition. It was the first time the Olympics were held in the Southern Hemisphere.

Trivia Answer: Michael Vick, with the Falcons (Colin Kaepernick would later top Vick's mark.)

DECEMBER

Today's Trivia: On December 2, 1985, what team handed the eventual Super Bowl champion Chicago Bears their lone loss of the NFL season?

Birthdays: Willie Brown, 1940; Ron Sutter, 1963; Chip Hale, 1964; Darryl Kile, 1968; O.J. McDuffie, 1969; Monica Seles, 1973; Mark Kotsay, 1975; Jason Collins, 1978; Aaron Rodgers, 1983; Brandon Knight, 1991; Sim Bhullar, 1992

On This Day: In 1975, Ohio State running back Archie Griffin was named the Heisman Trophy winner – for the second straight year. Griffin, the first player to start in four Rose Bowls, would become a first round pick of the Bengals in 1976. He remains the only man to win the Heisman twice.

Trivia Answer: Miami Dolphins, 38-24

DECEMBER

Today's Trivia: On December 3, 1993, what eventual NBA champions lost their first game of the season, to the Hawks, after opening with 15 straight wins?

Birthdays: Tom Fears, 1923; Bobby Allison, 1937; Alberto Juantorena, 1950; Rick Mears, 1951; Darryl Hamilton, 1964; Katarina Witt, 1965; Paul Byrd, 1970; Lindsey Hunter, 1970; James Laurinaitis, 1986

On This Day: In 1956, Wilt Chamberlain made his varsity debut at the University of Kansas, pouring in 52 points in a win over Northwestern. Ten years later to the day, Lew Alcindor (Kareem Abdul-Jabbar) gave UCLA basketball fans an idea of what was to come. Playing in his first varsity game for the Bruins, Alcindor scored 56 points in a win over USC.

Trivia Answer: Houston Rockets

DECEMBER

4

Today's Trivia: On December 4, 1997, the NBA suspended what Warriors All-Star for a full season following an incident in which he attacked head coach P.J. Carlesimo during a team practice?

Birthdays: Harvey Kuenn, 1930; Alex Delvecchio, 1932; Bernard King, 1956; Lee Smith, 1957; Frank Reich, 1961; Sergei Bubka, 1963; Jeff Blake, 1970; Tadahito Iguchi, 1974; Joe Thomas, 1984; Carlos Gomez, 1985; Martell Webster, 1986

On This Day: In 1977, the Tampa Bay Buccaneers walked the plank to their 26th consecutive loss, 10-0, to the Bears. After being shut out in four of their last five games, the expansion franchise's first win ever would come the following week against New Orleans – a 33-14 triumph.

Trivia Answer: Latrell Sprewell

DECEMBER

5

Today's Trivia: On December 5, 1981, the first college runner to gain over 2,000 yards in a season became the fourth USC back to win the Heisman Trophy in 16 years. Who is he?

Birthdays: Jim Plunkett, 1947; Lanny Wadkins, 1949; Jim Tressel, 1952; Muffet McGraw, 1955; Art Monk, 1957; Pablo Morales, 1964; Cliff Floyd, 1972; Charlie Batch, 1974; Eddy Curry, 1982; Josh Smith, 1985; LeGarrette Blount, 1986; A.J. Pollock, 1987; Christian Yelich, 1991

On This Day: In 1976, Bills running back O.J. Simpson ran for 200 yards for the sixth and final time of his NFL career. Exactly 32 years later, the Juice was sentenced to a maximum of 33 years in prison on charges of kidnapping and armed robbery. Simpson had led a group that broke into a Las Vegas hotel room and attempted to steal sports memorabilia.

Trivia Answer: Marcus Allen

DECEMBER

Today's Trivia: On December 6, 1984, Helena Sukova stopped whose record-winning streak of matches at 74 when she beat her in the semifinals of the Australian Open?

Birthdays: Tony Lazzeri, 1903; Stan Hack, 1909; Otto Graham, 1921; Andy Robustelli, 1925; Larry Bowa, 1945; Dwight Stones, 1953; Steve Bedrosian, 1957; Kevin Appier, 1967; Jose Contreras, 1971; Darrell Jackson, 1978; Robbie Gould, 1981; Adam Eaton, 1988; Johnny Manziel, 1992; Giannis Antetokounmpo, 1994

On This Day: In 2000, the Warriors defeated the Lakers in overtime, 125-122, in a historic contest. Kobe Bryant and Antawn Jamison each scored 51 points, marking the first time since the 1960s that opposing players reached 50 in the same game.

Trivia Answer: Martina Navratilova

DECEMBER

Today's Trivia: On December 7, 1980, what team pulled off the biggest regular season comeback in NFL history after trailing the Saints, 35-7, at halftime?

Birthdays: Bo Belinsky, 1936; Gerry Cheevers, 1940; Johnny Bench, 1947; Larry Bird, 1956; Ozzie Virgil, 1956; Shane Mack, 1963; Tino Martinez, 1967; Terrell Owens, 1973; Al Harris, 1974; Alan Faneca, 1976; Eric Chavez, 1977; Yasiel Puig, 1990

On This Day: In 1963, CBS unveiled a broadcast innovation during the Army-Navy game. The network used instant replay to showcase the many moves of the Midshipmen's scrambling quarterback, Roger Staubach. Staubach's team won, 21-15.

Trivia Answer: San Francisco 49ers, who won, 38-35

DECEMBER

8

Today's Trivia: On December 8, 1980, Howard Cosell delivered what tragic news to a *Monday Night Football* audience that was tuned in to watch the Dolphins vs. Patriots?

Birthdays: Red Berenson, 1939; Bob Brown, 1941; Bill Polian, 1942; George Rogers, 1958; Teresa Weatherspoon, 1965; Jeff George, 1967; Barry Foster, 1968; Mike Mussina, 1968; Kevin Harvick, 1975; Vernon Wells, 1978; Philip Rivers, 1981; Josh Donaldson, 1985; Dwight Howard, 1985; Sam Shields, 1987

On This Day: In 1940, Chicago crushed Washington, 73-0, in the NFL Championship Game. The Redskins had more passing yardage than the Bears and the same number of first downs, but Chicago pulled down eight interceptions. Just three weeks earlier, Washington had defeated Chicago, 7-3.

Trivia Answer: The death of John Lennon

DECEMBER

9

Today's Trivia: On December 9, 2004, Houston stunned the Spurs, 81-80, after what Rocket exploded for 13 points in the final 35 seconds of the game?

Birthdays: Cliff Hagan, 1931; Bill Hartack, 1932; Orville Moody, 1933; Deacon Jones, 1938; Dick Butkus, 1942; Tom Kite, 1949; World B. Free, 1953; Otis Birdsong, 1955; Jim Haslett, 1955; Al "Bubba" Baker, 1956; Juan Samuel, 1960; Tony Batista, 1973; David Akers, 1974; Gerald Henderson, 1987; Eric Bledsoe, 1989; McKayla Maroney, 1995

On This Day: In 1977, the Lakers' Kermit Washington sucker-punched Houston's Rudy Tomjanovich during a game, hospitalizing him with a fractured jaw and concussion, among other things. The disturbing incident resulted in a 26-game suspension for Washington and ended Rudy T's season.

Trivia Answer: Tracy McGrady

DECEMBER

10

Today's Trivia: On December 10, 1971, the Mets received Jim Fregosi, an All-Star who would last barely a year in New York, in a trade with the Angels. What pitcher did they deal to California to get him?

Birthdays: Ray Felix, 1930; Mark Aguirre, 1959; Paul Assenmacher, 1960; Luis Polonia, 1963; Rob Blake, 1969; Joe Mays, 1975; D'Brickashaw Ferguson, 1983; Matt Forte, 1985; Dion Waiters, 1991

On This Day: In 1989, Steve Largent became the first NFL player to catch 100 touchdown passes in a career. Exactly 17 years later, LaDainian Tomlinson scored his 29th TD of the year, topping the single-season mark recently set by Shaun Alexander. L.T. would finish with 31.

Trivia Answer: Nolan Ryan

DECEMBER

11

Today's Trivia: On December 11, 1993, what future NBA point guard was named the Heisman Trophy winner by one of the largest margins in the history of the voting?

Birthdays: Bill Nicholson, 1914; Doc Blanchard, 1924; Pierre Pilote, 1931; Del Shofner, 1934; Fred Cox, 1938; Karen Hantze Susman, 1942; Jay Bell, 1965; Derek Bell, 1968; Willie McGinest, 1971; Vonnie Holliday, 1975; Shareef Abdur-Rahim, 1976; Joe Blanton, 1980; Roman Harper, 1982; Roy Hibbert, 1986

On This Day: In 2000, Alex Rodriguez and the Texas Rangers agreed to a landmark 10-year deal worth $252 million. The contract was at the time the largest in sports history. A-Rod would last just three seasons in Texas before being dealt to the Yankees.

Trivia Answer: Charlie Ward, then a Florida State quarterback

DECEMBER

12

Today's Trivia: On December 12, 2015, the Golden State Warriors suffered their first loss of the season after opening an astounding 24-0. Who defeated them, 108-95?

Birthdays: Henry Armstrong, 1912; Bob Pettit, 1932; Emerson Fittipaldi, 1946; Billy Smith, 1950; Gorman Thomas, 1950; Cathy Rigby, 1952; Tracy Austin, 1962; Mike Golic, 1962; Haywood Jeffires, 1964; John Randle, 1967; Orlando Hudson, 1977; Ronnie Brown, 1981; Andrew Whitworth, 1981; Ervin Santana, 1982; T.J. Ward, 1986; Alfred Morris, 1988; Tyron Smith, 1990

On This Day: In 1965, two of the NFL's legendary running backs combined for eleven touchdowns. Paul Hornung scored five TDs in a Packers win over the Colts, while rookie Gale Sayers was even more productive with six scores in a Bears triumph over the 49ers.

Trivia Answer: Milwaukee Bucks

DECEMBER

13

Today's Trivia: On December 13, 2009, who set an NFL record with 21 receptions in one game against the Colts?

Birthdays: Archie Moore, 1913; Larry Doby, 1923; Carl Erskine, 1926; Ferguson Jenkins, 1942; Larry Kenon, 1952; Bob Gainey, 1953; Dale Berra, 1956; Richard Dent, 1960; Gary Zimmerman, 1961; Rex Ryan, 1962; Mike Tirico, 1966; Sergei Federov, 1969; Rickie Fowler, 1988; Fletcher Cox, 1990; Vladimir Tarasenko, 1991

On This Day: In 1983, the highest-scoring game in NBA history took place as the Pistons defeated the Nuggets, 186-184, in triple overtime. Among the contributors to the 370 combined points were Detroit's Isiah Thomas (47) and Denver's Kiki Vandeweghe (51) and Alex English (47).

Trivia Answer: Brandon Marshall, with the Broncos

DECEMBER

Today's Trivia: On December 14, 1991, less than a month after striking the Heisman pose when he scored on a punt return, who was named the Heisman Trophy winner in a runaway vote?

Birthdays: Charley Trippi, 1921; Ernie Davis, 1939; Stan Smith, 1946; Bill Buckner, 1949; Craig Biggio, 1965; Ken Hill, 1965; Anthony Mason, 1966; Scott Hatteberg, 1969; Dave Nilsson, 1969; Billy Koch, 1974; Nicolas Batum, 1988

On This Day: In 1988, the expansion Miami Heat enjoyed the thrill of victory for the first time, beating the L.A. Clippers, 89-88. The Heat had experienced the agony of defeat in 17 straight games before notching the franchise's initial NBA win. The Nets and 76ers now share the dubious distinction of 18 straight losses to begin a season.

Trivia Answer: Desmond Howard, from Michigan

DECEMBER

Today's Trivia: On December 15, 2002, what receiver caught nine passes to break Herman Moore's single-season NFL record of 123?

Birthdays: Joe Walton, 1935; Nick Buoniconti, 1940; Jim Leyland, 1944; Art Howe, 1946; Charlie Scott, 1948; Mo Vaughn, 1967; Rodney Harrison, 1972; Josh Norman, 1987; Jahlil Okafor, 1995

On This Day: In 1968, Philadelphia fans infamously booed Santa Claus as the Eagles hosted the Vikings at Franklin Field. The person hired to play Santa in a halftime parade was nowhere to be found. After a last-minute replacement was pulled from the stands, fans gave him the business as he took the field.

Trivia Answer: Marvin Harrison (He ended the season with 143.)

DECEMBER

16

Today's Trivia: On December 16, 1973, who became the first player in NFL history to rush for 2,000 yards in a single season?

Birthdays: Buddy Parker, 1913; Mike Flanagan, 1951; Bart Oates, 1958; Jeff Ruland, 1958; William "Refrigerator" Perry, 1962; Billy Ripken, 1964; Clifford Robinson, 1966; Donovan Bailey, 1967; Antrel Rolle, 1982; Alcides Escobar, 1986

On This Day: In 1930, golf's Bobby Jones became the first recipient of the Sullivan Award as "the outstanding amateur athlete in the United States." The honor, often referred to as the Oscar of sports awards, is named for Amateur Athletic Union founder James Edward Sullivan.

Trivia Answer: O.J. Simpson

DECEMBER

17

Today's Trivia: On December 17, 1995, the Browns played their last NFL game in Cleveland before moving to Baltimore for the following season. The event also marked the final game ever played at what venue?

Birthdays: Leo Cardenas, 1938; Peter Snell, 1938; Ken Hitchcock, 1951; Bob Ojeda, 1957; Eddie Brown, 1962; Vincent Damphousse, 1967; Chuck Liddell, 1969; Tony Richardson, 1971; Takeo Spikes, 1976; Manny Pacquiao, 1978; Chase Utley, 1978; Steve Weatherford, 1982; Buddy Hield, 1993

On This Day: In 1933, the NFL held its first Championship Game, at Chicago's Wrigley Field. The Bears, led by Bronko Nagurski, edged the New York Giants, 23-21.

Trivia Answer: Municipal Stadium (The Browns beat the Bengals, 26-10.)

DECEMBER

18

Today's Trivia: On December 18, 1959, Hall of Famer Sammy Baugh was named the first head coach of the New York Titans. The franchise began play the following season, and has been known since 1963 as the...what?

Birthdays: Ty Cobb, 1886; Bill Skowron, 1930; Gene Shue, 1931; Zoilo Versalles, 1939; Charles Oakley, 1963; Don Beebe, 1964; Arantxa Sanchez Vicario, 1971; Peter Boulware, 1974; Ben Watson, 1980; Byron Buxton, 1993

On This Day: In 1932, the first-ever NFL playoff game took place as the Chicago Bears defeated the Portsmouth Spartans, 9-0, for the title. After the two teams finished the year with identical records, the game was scheduled to determine the league champion.

Trivia Answer: New York Jets

DECEMBER

19

Today's Trivia: On December 19, 2010, the Eagles shocked the Giants in the "Miracle at the New Meadowlands". After trailing by 21 with under eight minutes to play, Philly came back to tie it. What Eagle then won the game on a walk-off punt return TD as time expired?

Birthdays: Bobby Layne, 1926; Al Kaline, 1934; Kevin McHale, 1957; Reggie White, 1961; Bill Wegman, 1962; Randall McDaniel, 1964; Arvydas Sabonis, 1964; Tom Gugliotta, 1969; Warren Sapp, 1972; Jake Plummer, 1974; Russell Branyan, 1975; Rafael Soriano, 1979; Mo Williams, 1982; Ian Kennedy, 1984

On This Day: In 1984, the Buffalo Sabres beat the Chicago Blackhawks, 6-3, making Scotty Bowman the NHL's all-time winningest coach. It was the 691st victory of Bowman's career, which started with St. Louis. He would finish up with Detroit, retiring with over 1,200 regular season victories.

Trivia Answer: DeSean Jackson

DECEMBER

20

Today's Trivia: On December 20, 2005, what player outscored the Dallas Mavericks through three quarters by himself, 62-61, before sitting the entire fourth of a blowout win?

Birthdays: Branch Rickey, 1881; Fred Merkle, 1888; Gabby Hartnett, 1900; Bob Hayes, 1942; Bo Ryan, 1947; Cecil Cooper, 1949; Bill Clement, 1950; Nate Newton, 1961; Rich Gannon, 1965; Bobby Phills, 1969; Aubrey Huff, 1976; James Shields, 1981; David Wright, 1982; Martavis Bryant, 1991

On This Day: In 1980, NBC broadcast a game between the Jets and Dolphins without announcers. Viewers were aided by graphics and the stadium's public address system in this one-time experiment. Exactly 23 years later, an inebriated Joe Namath appeared alongside ESPN sideline reporter Suzy Kolber. Unfortunately for Broadway Joe, there was plenty of audio for this Jets-Patriots game.

Trivia Answer: Kobe Bryant

DECEMBER

21

Today's Trivia: On December 21, 2007, the Cincinnati Reds dealt what future MVP to the Texas Rangers after his first season in the Major Leagues?

Birthdays: Josh Gibson, 1911; Joe Paterno, 1926; Dave Kingman, 1948; Joaquin Andujar, 1952; Chris Evert, 1954; Tom Henke, 1957; Florence Griffith Joyner, 1959; Andy Van Slyke, 1960; Terry Mills, 1967; LaTroy Hawkins, 1972; Mike Alstott, 1973; Karrie Webb, 1974; Freddy Sanchez, 1977; Philip Humber, 1982; Mark Ingram, 1989; Ha Ha Clinton-Dix, 1992

On This Day: In 1891, 18 students played in the first game of basketball based off of James Naismith's set of published rules. Exactly 90 years later, Cincinnati pulled out a 75-73 win over Bradley in seven overtimes, the longest college basketball game in history.

Trivia Answer: Josh Hamilton

DECEMBER

Today's Trivia: On December 22, 1985, what 49er became the first player in NFL history to gain 1,000 yards both rushing and receiving in the same season?

Birthdays: Connie Mack, 1862; Matty Alou, 1938; Steve Carlton, 1944; Steve Garvey, 1948; Ray Guy, 1949; Jan Stephenson, 1951; Lonnie Smith, 1955; Zach Britton, 1987

On This Day: In 1946, Otto Graham led his Cleveland Browns to a 14-9 victory over the New York Yankees at Cleveland Stadium in the first All-America Football Conference Championship Game. The Browns would win all four of the AAFC's titles before the league disbanded and they were admitted to the NFL for the 1950 season.

Trivia Answer: Roger Craig (Marshall Faulk has since joined him.)

DECEMBER

Today's Trivia: On December 23, 1982, tiny Chaminade pulled off one of college basketball's biggest upsets when they took down what top-ranked team led by All-American center Ralph Sampson?

Birthdays: Dick Weber, 1929; Paul Hornung, 1935; Willie Wood, 1936; Jerry Koosman, 1942; Bill Rodgers, 1947; Jack Ham, 1948; Jerry Manuel, 1953; Jim Harbaugh, 1963; Greg Biffle, 1969; Brad Lidge, 1976; Alge Crumpler, 1977; Victor Martinez, 1978; Johan Franzen, 1979; Scott Gomez, 1979; Cody Ross, 1980; Hanley Ramirez, 1983

On This Day: In 1972, Franco Harris made the "Immaculate Reception" that advanced the Steelers to the AFC Championship Game. Trailing the Raiders, 7-6, with under 30 seconds to go, Terry Bradshaw threw a fourth-down desperation pass. The throw bounced off an Oakland defender and into the hands of Harris, who ran 42 yards for the winning score.

Trivia Answer: Virginia, 77-72

DECEMBER

24

Today's Trivia: On December 24, 1977, one of the most famous plays in NFL history transpired as the Raiders defeated the Colts in a classic double overtime playoff game. Who did Oakland QB Ken Stabler hit on a 42-yard "Ghost to the Post" play to keep his team alive?

Birthdays: Bill Dudley, 1921; Paul Pressey, 1958; Kevin Millwood, 1974; Jamey Wright, 1974; Gregor Blanco, 1983; Tim Jennings, 1983; Davante Adams, 1992

On This Day: In 1967, Joe Namath became the first quarterback in NFL history to throw for 4,000 yards in a single season, doing so in a 14-game season. He reached the mark with 343 yards passing in a win against the Chargers. Namath's feat would not be matched for another 12 years, when Dan Fouts joined him.

Trivia Answer: Dave Casper

DECEMBER

25

Today's Trivia: On December 25, 1984, what Knick poured in 60 points in a Christmas Day loss to the Nets at Madison Square Garden?

Birthdays: Nellie Fox, 1927; Lefty Driesell, 1931; Ken Stabler, 1945; Larry Csonka, 1946; Manny Trillo, 1950; Hanford Dixon, 1958; Rickey Henderson, 1958; Hideki Okajima, 1975; Marcus Trufant, 1980; Demaryius Thomas, 1987; Eric Gordon, 1988

On This Day: In 1971, Miami and Kansas City played the NFL's longest game. The outcome wasn't decided until the Dolphins' Garo Yepremian kicked a 37-yard field goal more than 22 minutes into sudden-death overtime. Miami advanced in the playoffs with the 27-24 win.

Trivia Answer: Bernard King

DECEMBER

Today's Trivia: On December 26, 1908, who defeated Tommy Burns in a bout in Australia to became the first-ever black heavyweight champion?

Birthdays: Glenn Davis, 1924; Stu Miller, 1927; Bill Yeoman, 1927; Norm Ullman, 1935; Carlton Fisk, 1947; Chris Chambliss, 1948; Ozzie Smith, 1954; Tim Legler, 1966; Marcelo Rios, 1975; Omar Infante, 1981; Yohan Blake, 1989; Chris Borland, 1990

On This Day: In 1960, Philadelphia's Chuck Bednarik stopped Jim Taylor near the 10-yard line as time expired in the NFL Championship Game, preserving a 17-13 win over the Packers. Exactly five years later, Buffalo defeated the Chargers for a second consecutive time in the AFL Championship Game. Neither the Eagles nor Bills have won a title since.

Trivia Answer: Jack Johnson

DECEMBER

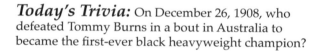

Today's Trivia: On December 27, 1967, the man who is honored with "613" hanging from the Madison Square Garden rafters was hired to become the head coach of the New York Knicks. Who is he?

Birthdays: Nolan Richardson, 1941; Roy White, 1943; Andre Tippett, 1959; Bill Self, 1962; Jim Leyritz, 1963; Dean Palmer, 1968; Kevin Ollie, 1972; Deuce McAllister, 1978; Carson Palmer, 1979; Michael Bourn, 1982; Cole Hamels, 1983; Jamaal Charles, 1986; Rick Porcello, 1988

On This Day: In 2000, Mario Lemieux came out of retirement as the Penguins took on the Maple Leafs. In his first NHL action since 1997, Lemieux didn't miss a beat, tallying a goal and three points in his team's win. The Magnificent One would hang up his skates for good in 2006.

Trivia Answer: Red Holzman (The "613" represents his number of wins with the Knicks.)

DECEMBER

28

Today's Trivia: On December 28, 1975, a new football term was coined when the Cowboys beat the Vikings in a playoff game on a last-second 50-yard touchdown pass. On the miracle score, what quarterback said, "I closed my eyes and said a Hail Mary"?

Birthdays: Steve Van Buren, 1920; Terry Sawchuk, 1929; Bill Lee, 1946; Ray Knight, 1952; Everson Walls, 1959; Ray Bourque, 1960; Adam Vinatieri, 1972; B.J. Ryan, 1975; James Blake, 1979; Bill Hall, 1979; Cedric Benson, 1982

On This Day: In 1958, the NFL Championship was decided in sudden death for the first time. Alan Ameche's touchdown run after eight minutes of overtime gave the Colts a 23-17 win over the Giants at Yankee Stadium in what has been dubbed "The Greatest Game Ever Played."

Trivia Answer: Roger Staubach (Drew Pearson was on the receiving end of the throw.)

DECEMBER

29

Today's Trivia: On December 29, 2007, the New England Patriots finished off a perfect 16-0 regular season in what was an otherwise-meaningless game for the teams involved. Who did they take down, 38-35?

Birthdays: Jim Murray, 1919; Ray Nitschke, 1936; Wayne Huizenga, 1937; Laffit Pincay Jr., 1946; Devon White, 1962; Sean Payton, 1963; Jay Fiedler, 1971; Theo Epstein, 1973; Richie Sexson, 1974; Jaret Wright, 1975; Laveranues Coles, 1977; Jack Wilson, 1977; Eric Berry, 1988; Travis Benjamin, 1989

On This Day: In 1978, Ohio State lost the Gator Bowl and their head coach. After a Clemson interception, Buckeyes coach Woody Hayes erupted and punched the Tiger player who picked off the ball. Hayes was relieved of his duties by the university. Four years later to the day, Alabama's Bear Bryant had a less tumultuous final game, as his Crimson Tide defeated Illinois in the Liberty Bowl.

Trivia Answer: New York Giants, who would later upset the Pats in the Super Bowl

DECEMBER

Today's Trivia: On December 30, 1907, the Mills Commission declared that the game of baseball was invented by what Civil War general?

Birthdays: Sandy Koufax, 1935; Jim Marshall, 1937; Mel Renfro, 1941; Jim Nance, 1942; Ben Johnson, 1961; Kerry Collins, 1972; Tiger Woods, 1975; A. J. Pierzynski, 1976; Laila Ali, 1977; Grant Balfour, 1977; Kenyon Martin, 1977; LeBron James, 1984; Carson Wentz, 1992

On This Day: In 1990, Orlando guard Scott Skiles dished out 30 assists to set an NBA record in a 155-116 win over Denver. He registered his last assist with 20 seconds left in the game. Skiles also added 22 points and six rebounds in his game for the ages.

Trivia Answer: Abner Doubleday (Skepticism remains about the true role Doubleday had in creating the game.)

DECEMBER

Today's Trivia: On December 31, 1988, the Bears defeated the Eagles in a Divisional Playoff contest that became known by what name because of the extreme weather conditions at Soldier Field?

Birthdays: Hugh McElhenny, 1928; Don James, 1932; Cliff Richey, 1946; Rick Aguilera, 1961; Bryon Russell, 1970; Brent Barry, 1971; Esteban Loaiza, 1971; Heath Shuler, 1971; Jason Campbell, 1981; Kelvin Herrera, 1989; Gabby Douglas, 1995

On This Day: In 1967, Bart Starr's one-yard plunge with 13 seconds remaining gave the Packers a 21-17 win over the Dallas Cowboys in the "Ice Bowl" for their third straight NFL title. Over 50,000 fans braved well-below-zero temperatures at Green Bay's Lambeau Field.

Trivia Answer: The Fog Bowl